MW01673434

The Music of an Untuned Mind

A Neurologist Reharmonizes His Mind after Crashing in Africa

AVI ERLICH, PHD, MD

Copyright © 2021 by Avi Erlich

All rights reserved. No part of this publication may be reproduced, distributed, or transmitted in any form or by any means, including photocopying, recording, or other electronic or mechanical methods, without the prior written permission of the publisher, except in the case of brief quotations embodied in critical reviews and certain other noncommercial uses permitted by copyright law.

Redwood Publishing, LLC
Orange County, California
info@redwooddigitalpublishing.com

Printed in the United States of America

First Printing, 2021

Disclaimer: This book is designed to provide information and motivation to its readers. It is sold with the understanding that the author and publisher are not engaged to render any type of psychological, legal, or any other kind of professional advice. The content of each article is the sole expression and opinion of its author and is not meant to substitute for any advice from your healthcare professionals, lawyers, therapists, business advisors/partners, or personal connections.

978-1-952106-95-8 - Paperback
978-1-952106-96-5 - Ebook

Library of Congress Control Number: 2021905890

Cover Design: Graphique Designs, LLC
Cover Photograph: ID 83336949 © Pv Productions | Dreamstime.com
Interior Design: Jose Pepito

First Edition

10 9 8 7 6 5 4 3 2 1

For my physicians,

Dr. Kathleen Bell

Dr. Kurt Johnson

And for my children,

Shala, Aaron, Margaret

My art is not past power nor you past cure.

— William Shakespeare, *All's Well That Ends Well,* act 2, scene 1

Order must be discovered and, in a deep sense, it must be created. What we see, as we see it, is mere disorder.

— J. Bronowski, *Science and Human Values*

Contents

CHAPTER ONE

Bad Accidents

Even the helpless victim of a hopeless situation, facing a fate he cannot change, may rise above himself, may grow beyond himself, and by so doing change himself. He may turn a personal tragedy into a triumph.

– Viktor E. Frankl, *Man's Search for Meaning*

CALL ME A BOOKISH MAN: A FORMER PROFESSOR OF ENGLISH LITERATURE, then a neurologist, run over by a milk truck at age four in Los Angeles, suffering fractures and scars—my left elbow crushed and my forearm shortened for life. In the hospital for a month, I was carried out broken by my father. And then, after a long period of vigorous good health, I suffered another life-changing accident: a bicycle wreck in Kenya at age sixty-six. I had multiple fractures on the left side of my body, including my pelvis, nine of my ribs, my collarbone, and my skull, with associated brain injury. I have no memory of how this more recent accident occurred, and there were no witnesses. The British organizers of my bike tour thought that I might have been struck by a wildebeest. Eventually, I went back to work, having spent three months in the hospital on three separate continents.

My interest in these accidents lies not simply in the connections between them, but also in their power to shape and enrich my "normal life." Without integrating the accidental with the purposeful, I would not be able to live deeply or practice the art of medicine. By reviewing and recomposing memories of past trauma, I sharpened my aesthetic sensibility. The activation of this universal capacity to weave together old memories and current suffering has a healing power. "Only connect," wrote the English novelist E. M. Forster. "Live in fragments no longer."

To interpret a poem, to pull together all the surface detail and plumb its underlying theme, is much like the practice of medicine, which requires a weaving together of a patient's symptoms and the results of his physical examination—a piercing of the fog of detail, a "knowing through," which is plain English for the Greek-derived *diagnosis*. This is the physician's task, to know and understand. But sometimes the patient has to find a way to muster the same art. Healing from traumatic brain injury, I belatedly learned, requires a reintegration, a calling on the brain's plasticity, an application of the brain's own creative energies to weave itself back together.

As I lay in the Brain Injury unit of the University of Washington Rehabilitation Center, I could do nothing other than activate my lifelong urge to create, to produce a patterned tapestry of greater meaning than the sum of its unwoven threads. And this, in turn actually—and surprisingly—facilitated my recovery from my crash in Kenya. Though I have painted all my life, I did not know, even as a neurologist, that the drive to compose both arises from and helps repair the physical weave of the brain. The human brain creates art, and the creation of art can help repair the injured brain. Human brains create art for a reason.

My plan for this book is to show how I helped heal myself by drawing on my memories of prior trauma, and the even larger web of relationships that come into play when one becomes badly damaged and despondent. These old memories helped me remake myself, just as they had in the past. On each occasion, I drew from a refreshed palette, recomposing my thoughts and thus my mind.

I could not use memories of the more recent accident itself, for I had none. I remember looking for a missing bicycle glove that morning at an ostrich farm where we had camped, but I can recall neither the crash nor the first three hospitals to which I was later admitted. As a neurologist who treats patients with memory loss, I had to take care of myself by using what memories I had, fashioning from them a usable story. And that story, this book, helped construct a necessary web of new connections in my brain. The woven tale is the outer dressing of the inner rehabilitation.

I discovered for myself that the human capacity for aesthetics has the power to heal an injured brain, but this is an old idea, as in a painting by Louis Ducis, *Sappho Recalled to Life by the Charm of*

Music (circa 1811), which I regarded with new interest in the Norton Simon Museum in Pasadena after I recovered.

The legend of the poet Sappho tells us that her art was restored by the administration of art. This well composed canvas itself helped to heal me.

Every hospital ward for the treatment of traumatic brain injury or dementia or psychiatric disturbance offers art therapy. The clinical justification for this is described in Noah Hass-Cohen and Joanna Clyde Findlay's *Art Therapy and Clinical Neuroscience*. "Art therapy seems poised to enable," say these authors, "positive therapeutic changes while possibly enhancing synaptic plasticity and creating multi-tiered psychological outcomes." But no good clinical or laboratory evidence supports this optimistic claim. It is clear that a well-woven brain creates art, because that's what brains do in every human culture we know. But does art help recreate brain? Can the remains of artful thinking help the injured brain rewire its disconnected neurons?

The kind of evidence we need to answer this question is not in theory impossible to acquire, given the rapid improvement of functional imaging of the brain. If creative thinking can make positive changes in the anatomy of human memory, this might be demonstrable. While we wait for this technology to mature, let me offer an example of the creativity that is already wired into the brain of a toddler. My eighteen-month-old granddaughter, Perri, composed this:

Is there not something more here than the product of a babyish urge to scribble? Do we not see the expression of a sense of perspective and balance? Is this not a demonstration of a developing brain composed to compose?

When I was a child, a bit older than Perri, I took cooling charcoal out of our barbeque in Los Angeles and drew on the outer walls of our house, beginning with abstract scenes and progressing to mountains, trees, and lakes. I attended to the rules of perspective, driven by those of my neurons that were organized to compose. All my life, I have employed art to master trauma.

Although we may have no direct evidence that art therapy, including written composition, helps recompose neural tissue after injury, we do have clinical experience that demonstrates that exercising a patient's inborn creativity improves recovery after stroke and other brain injuries. In *Mended by the Muse: Creative Transformations of Trauma*, Sophia Richman summarizes her case: "While all forms of artistic expression can be instrumental in self-healing, writing is particularly well suited for the integration of cognitive and emotional aspects if self, especially when it is autobiographical."

Without thinking much about what I was doing, I turned inward during my recovery to recreate myself by writing about my own memories. I am blessed with a strong visual memory, almost photographic when I was young (I could close my eyes and count the tines of a comb I had just seen), and I found that by writing about old visions, I could make progress toward returning to myself. How this may have rearranged my brain I do not know, but I will later speculate on the therapeutic changes in my brain's apparatus that I might have set in motion.

While undergoing rehabilitation, I recalled that at the age of three, I had walked with my mother through the neighborhood of Venice in Southern California to the canals that had been dug to mimic those in Venice, Italy. My mother told me that the developer had run out of money (she had to explain what she'd meant by "gone broke," an expression I'd thought literal and terrifying), so the planned palazzos had never been built.

On the following day, the Sabbath, after an unusually heavy rain, I dressed myself in the nice clothes my mother had laid out for me and wandered out of our tract house, which my father had bought for $3,500 under the GI Bill. In our small yard, I picked up a small trowel and headed for the abandoned farm at the dead-end of our street, Commonwealth Avenue, to the place we called the "Bean Field." I carefully dug a canal to redirect a large puddle of water, and then returned home filthy, much to my mother's displeasure.

"Don't you know, it's Shabbat; you have to stay clean and do no work!" she scolded.

But I was pleased that I had crafted order out of a muddy mess, a canal where future houses could be built.

As I tell my story, I present my material both as a neurologist, drawing on relevant neuroscience, and as a literary man, having earned a PhD in English at the University of California, Berkeley, which led to the publication of my thesis, *Hamlet's Absent Father.* I now have in mind a tale in the genre of Oliver Sacks' *A Leg to*

Stand On. Fearing he would be gored, Dr. Sacks, a neurologist at my medical school, fled from a bull that he encountered while hiking on a mountain in Norway. He fell, severing his left femoral nerve, which left his quadriceps—the thigh muscles, the most powerful in the body—marooned. Unable to walk, he scooted along on his buttocks, using his umbrella as a punting pole, until he could no longer move. After he had given up hope, another hiker found him just at dusk and rescued him from freezing to death.

But his recovery was not easy. His injured leg convinced his brain that it was an alien object, and so he summoned his nurse to have it removed from his bed. In his persistent state of paralysis, confusion, and despondency, he drew on his literary skills to recover both his mind and body. His trauma aroused the very capacity he needed most, his own self-administered art therapy.

Of course, creativity is not always sufficient to reweave an injured brain, as is demonstrated by the case of Jean-Dominique Bauby. The former editor of the French fashion magazine *Elle* suffered a brain stem stroke that rendered him locked in, able to think but unable to move a single muscle except his left eyelid. Unlike Dr. Sacks, he did not survive. Nevertheless, he managed to blink his story to an amanuensis via a code that he developed. He finished blinking *Le scaphandre et le papillon* (*The Diving Bell and the Butterfly*), and then he expired, having revealed the winged mind of a man who could collect, preserve, and reweave his memories, despite being locked into his own glass coffin, his diving bell. The man, the mind, and the miserable stroke of bad luck melded. Bauby remained artful as long as life sustained his creative brain.

My bad luck in Kenya, having rendered me a brain-injured

neurologist, reawakened memories of old traumas and recoveries. This time, I composed new music out of old cacophonous memories. I made them chime with a newly invigorated love of life and the affection of friends. What my brain wove together was beneficent, not because its parts were lovely, but because they were harmonized, composed so that the ugliness of the parts was tempered.

The injured brain is a jangle of circuits, a skein of tangled yarn. The recovering brain's rewoven neurons revive the capacity for coherence, for creativity, for harmony. The music of the mind is the basis for the human aesthetic impulse, present in every culture and in every age. The French say, "*Chaque langue a sa musique*," every language has its own music. And, one should add, every human brain has its own individualized music, especially when healthy.

Injured brains tend to repeat the same nonsense in a repetitive, cacophonous babble, the cure for which is the restoration of the healthy harmony of the brain. T. S. Eliot put it this way: "You are the music while the music lasts." And the German poet Novalis, writing at the time of Keats, phrased it like this: "Every disease is a musical problem; every cure is a musical solution." That music is my subject because it has neurologic causes and neurologic effects. The history of art and music is one with the history of mind.

In the prepared mind, the accidental, be it disastrous or miraculous, can bring its own blessings. Neurologists speak of the brain's plasticity, its power to remake itself, to heal itself after injury or failure. We tend to trivialize this healing plasticity, forgetting the Greek origin of the word *plastic*. *Plastikos* means fit for molding.

Plaster of Paris is that material from which both a sculpture and a healing cast can be molded. When speaking of the brain's plasticity, we have much more in mind than cheap plastic.

We now know that the brain's plasticity, its ability to change strategies, its capacity for learning through trial and error, its ability to pull together all factors relevant to the moment in order to remake itself by getting a new grip, constitutes what we call the human brain's executive function, which resides in the prefrontal cortex, in health and in an injured state. In *The New Executive Brain*, Elkhonon Goldberg summarizes the relevant neuro-anatomy of plasticity and executive function. "Of all the structures in the brain, only the prefrontal cortex is embedded in . . . a richly networked pattern of neural pathways. This unique connectivity makes the frontal lobes singularly suited for coordinating and integrating the work of all the other brain structures—the conductor of the orchestra," the harmonizer.

Others have expanded on Dr. Goldberg's observations. "Neuroplastic approaches," writes Dr. Norman Doidge, "require the active involvement of the whole patient in his or her own care: mind, brain, and body." Despite the terror of being admitted to rehab with a diagnosis of traumatic brain injury, I made every effort to push myself into Doidge's world, at first grasping at strange and flimsy straws. Eventually, I rediscovered my own capacity to create and recreate.

CHAPTER TWO

A Cycling Tour in Kenya

And what if the idea of truly restoring patients meant not only achieving the absence of pain but nothing less than bringing them back to a fuller life?

– Norman Doidge, *The Brain's Way of Healing*

MY SON, AARON, IS A RESTLESS, INTELLIGENT YOUNG MAN, SAID TO BE much like his father. After high school, he mastered Spanish while trekking the length of Latin America before obtaining degrees at Dartmouth College and Georgetown University. Then he lived in Barcelona, where he became a certified teacher of

English as a foreign language. This led to a job in Bratislava, where he learned Slovakian. After that, he went off to Moscow, where he became fluent in Russian, picking up German along the way. With no clear goal in mind, he then worked for four years in Soviet Georgia, helping to develop democracy, thus earning by chance a consultancy in Kenya. His mind roamed further and further afield, running to or from something that was unclear to both him and me.

Yearly we set out on long cycling trips—along the Saint Lawrence River from Quebec City, over the Southern Alps on the South Island of New Zealand, through the old Muscovite capitals around Moscow. We biked the back roads of Bulgaria to old monasteries and Turkish forts. When I lagged behind on mountain ascents, burdened with panniers, he twiddled his thumbs at the top of passes, partly for amusement and partly to flaunt his superior prowess.

Because Aaron was working in Nairobi in 2011, I signed us up for a British bicycle tour from Nairobi to Dar es Salaam, Arabic for "home of peace," which just happens to be the name of the cemetery in Los Angeles where my parents and grandparents are buried. I was born in the City of Angels at the end of WWII, just in time to hear about the war from returning vets and their families. My father fought Nazis in the snow at the Battle of the Bulge. His feet froze in the field, putting him in a military hospital in Frankfurt and leaving him with a frozen soul. He lived on as a disconnected man.

I am not easily intimidated, nor am I one who believes in premonitions, for I am a physician, immersed in the science of medicine, eschewing humbug, the founder of the first stroke program in Seattle. So I was not going to heed my deep misgivings about cycling to Dar es Salaam. My friend and colleague Dr. David

Warth said to me on one of his visits to my hospital room on the Rehabilitation ward at the University of Washington Medical Center, "I remember you telling me the day before you left that you shouldn't go on this trip." My friend Marie-Louise Mercer recalled that I had spoken similarly to her.

I arrived in Nairobi a few days before the bike tour so that I could do a little sightseeing. Moses, the driver whom Aaron used regularly, took us first to the former home of Karen Blixen. I had read her famous book *Out of Africa* as an undergraduate at Berkeley in 1963, excited by the prospect that I, too, could lead an intelligent life of adventure. Perhaps I could get as far as Africa and flourish in a life of creative splendor, as did Isak Dinesen (*nom de plume* of Ms. Blixen), who lived with her husband, a baron who had their African mansion built by a Swedish architect. As I concentrated on building all kinds of mental mansions, I repressed the fact that the baron fatally crashed his small plane near his estate.

Moses next drove us to Nairobi's Giraffe Center, just down the road from Ms. Dinesen's museum.

Close-up, the gangly giraffe rivals Kandinsky, whose painting I admired in the Tretyakov Gallery in Moscow, which I visited with Aaron just before we cycled the Golden Ring, those beautiful capitals of medieval Russia. These monuments to chaos were built serially and without success to evade the marauding Mongols. Kandinsky also built beautiful monuments to chaos:

A human aesthetic impulse drives us to create order from disorder. I can see no other reason why people should line up to see a showing of Kandinsky's paintings. After seeing the giraffes, Moses drove Aaron and me—oh, the sweet pleasure of being escorted in Africa by Aaron and Moses, so prominent in the story of Passover—to a new, foreign-financed school in Nairobi

hovering just above one of the city's many slums. From a distance, the squalor resembled a Cézanne, something like *La Montagne Sainte Victoire.*

The slum should not be sentimentalized, but the photo has beauty, via craft and an accident of photography.

Then we came to our bike tour. Moses sent us on our way. The first day, I fell gently and without injury; the bike, stuck in mud, toppled me over at zero velocity. On the second day, as we cycled south on the African savanna, Aaron was in front of me on a flat dirt road, without traffic. Then we started downhill, the rest of the tour group ten minutes behind. Aaron took this photo:

I have no memory of what happened next, or of what transpired over the next two months. During the third month after the accident, I awoke in the Rehabilitation ward in Seattle, where I had recently been transferred from the university's Harborview Medical Center, a celebrated center for acute trauma. With no understanding of where I was, a memory of the evening before my crash popped into my mind. A game warden opened a gate so that I could see up close a single regal ostrich, taller than I, taking his evening stroll.

"Be careful," said the warden. "Do not get too close. He is not a little bird; he attacks and bites."

And suddenly, there before me in the present, were Aaron and Margaret standing at my bedside, smiling wanly.

"Where am I, and what happened to me?" I asked, bewildered. I was pleased to be in the presence of my children, but also terrified.

From Aaron, I learned that the oldest member of our ill-fated tour, a seventy-four-year-old pharmacist from Belgium, came across me as I lay delirious, bleeding from my head, my bike and helmet mysteriously intact, though the straps of the helmet were soaked with blood. The good pharmacist sped ahead, found Aaron (perhaps twiddling his thumbs), handing over to him the nightmare of figuring out what to do with me and arousing in him the power to focus his intelligence and immense ability. Nobody witnessed the accident.

Early speculation by the guides, said Aaron, included theories that I had been hit by a vehicle (but nobody had seen recent traffic) or knocked down by a wildebeest (although I fell in a known crossing, there were no signs that wildebeests had crossed recently). No satisfactory explanation ever emerged.

My own theory is that I reacted inappropriately to some warning of danger. My British tour company's mountain bike sported reversed brakes, in line with the English custom of driving on the wrong side of the road. The right brake controlled the front wheel, and the left, the rear—the reverse of the American setup. Further, I had just started taking Malarone, an anti-malaria prophylactic. I had asked Aaron, who had already taken the drug on three occasions, if he had experienced any side effects, and he'd said, "No." Foolishly, I, the experienced physician, never looked up the drug's possible adverse effects, which commonly include confusion and hallucinations. I could have consulted the Belgian pharmacist, but this wisdom never occurred to me. And I could have had the brakes reconfigured to the American standard, but I didn't.

I have ridden bicycles for more than fifty years over mountains and for long distances without problems. I've always been cautious, never a thrill-seeker, enjoying moving under my own power through beautiful or interesting country. In Russia, an oligarch warned me not to cycle because "either our police or our criminals will beat you and take your bicycles, money, and passports." Aaron and I did cycle, 116 miles on one day, into the Russian white night on rough roads, without serious mishaps, sometimes stuck in mud, but never struck, except by the beauty of Russian churches, many in ruins.

I suspected from what Aaron had told me, that on the bike in Kenya, I'd needed to stop abruptly, which would require a firm squeeze of the back brake. Braking a fast-moving bicycle with force to the front wheel will throw the rider headfirst over the handlebars, which is what I probably did, confused by Malarone. This was my best integration of the facts then known to me, crafted in a quiet but desperate attempt to master the terror of being amnesic about the relevant details. The ability to spin *any* explanation is itself a comfort.

My favorite physical therapist at the UW Medical Center, Vicky Stevens, showed me a clip on YouTube of a cyclist in a race on the African savannah being leveled broadside by a hurtling wildebeest, its four legs high off the ground, hooves poised at the level of the cyclist's head, antlers in position to butt. After shaking off the blow, the rider stood up, dazed—to me, an enviable outcome. Vicky, whose name was what my mother called me as a child, was reprimanded for showing me this video, for it was thought too unsettling for a brain-injured neurologist who himself had been knocked down on a bike in Africa. But it was useful for me, for it became part of my weave.

With the help of the tour guides, Aaron made his way to a distant hilltop, where emergency help could be summoned by cell phone. A helicopter was dispatched. It got lost for two hours, showing up eventually to fly me away, an event of which I still have no memory. My noble friend Marie-Louise, originally British but raised in Africa, wired $10,000 from Seattle to pay the rescue squad. I was intubated in the hospital in Nairobi and transferred a week later by air ambulance to London, where Sir Michael Marmot—an esteemed epidemiologist and a friend from our days at Berkeley—met Margaret at my new hospital. He took her to his home in Hampstead Heath, to his lovely wife, Alexi, a talented architect.

After two weeks of care in London, I was transferred by air

ambulance to Seattle—this time, a solo passenger, for there was no extra room, given all the medical equipment. I was on the ventilator for a total of thirty days, not extubated until I was ready to be transferred from Harborview Hospital to the main campus of UW Hospital, where I woke from a diet of opiates, mercifully being tapered down.

I arrived at UW Rehab on September 15. My first accomplishment at rehab was inscribed on my room's whiteboard: "On September 22, he ate." This, apparently, was an accomplishment worth noting after seven days of rehab. A slender nasogastric feeding tube was left in my left nostril for weeks. One night, I pulled the damned thing out in my sleep, apparently by accident, and was relieved to learn that it would not be replaced.

In my reawakened state, Aaron was able to show me on his laptop the CT scan of my head, taken in Nairobi the day after my accident. It showed a crack in my skull behind my left ear and a sprinkling of various hemorrhagic complications of traumatic head injury, with blood between the folds of my brain and in tiny dots within the brain itself.

On Aaron's laptop, I also saw images of my fractured pelvis, the left side looking like dog kibble. The view of my nine rib fractures did not bother me, as I had no conscious memory of the writhing pain that made me squirm constantly, causing my doctors in Harborview, according to Aaron, to medicate me into oblivion and nickname me "Doctor Wiggleworm." On the CT of my head, I could also see that the right side of my brain was swollen (the right side is on the viewer's left, as I am lying on my back, forehead up, with my feet toward the viewer). Normal gyri and ventricles (the brain's folds and pouches) are visible on the left, not on the right. Swelling effaces the right lateral ventricle, but the left remains normal, appearing as a black boomerang-like slit. The ghostly white dots and streaks on the right represent blood.

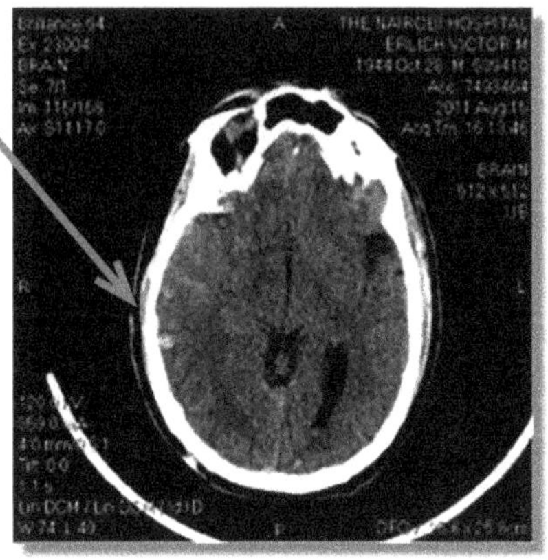

Galen, the famed Greco-Roman physician, thought the fluid sloshing in the ventricles was the abode of the soul, based on his dissection of monkey brains. I knew I was no monkey, but I recalled that the enraged Othello, brain-damaged by Iago, exclaimed, "Goats and monkeys!" And did I not lose my soul when the cerebrospinal fluid was squeezed out of my right cerebral ventricle?

The new crack in my left skull can be seen in the lower right corner of the image below, which shows my skull, via what we call the CT's "bone windows."

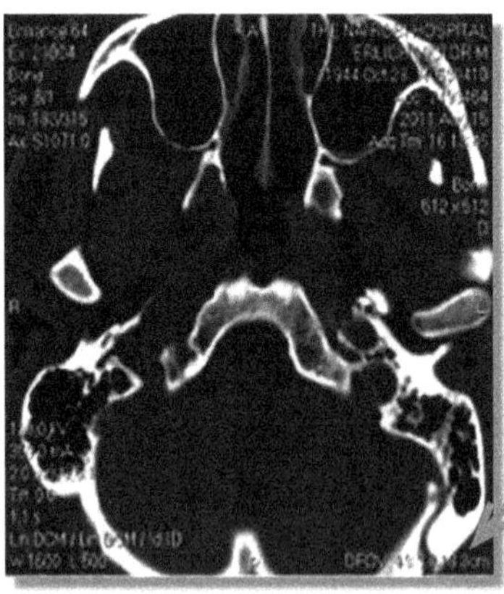

This fracture behind my left ear was probably a traumatic reopening of the lambdoid fissure, a normal gap that allows the infant's brain to grow, naturally sealing itself by the age of one. This new fracture might have deafened me, had I not already lost hearing in that ear from infantile mumps.

A CT slice lower down, through my cerebellum, showed a white drop of blood in the right cerebellar hemisphere and a black streak of swelling.

At first glance, this didn't appear very serious, but I knew that this injured part of my cerebellum coordinated much activity in my brain, fine-tuning the rhythm of my speech, the movement of my limbs and eyes, and the organization of my thinking. I was not far off the mark when I feared that I was suffering from cerebellar-frontal syndrome, that failure of the cerebellum to coordinate thought in such a way as to make action mesh with time and tide. This impairment of what we call executive function would rattle the way I presented myself and force me to repeat myself in the futile hope of making myself understood. Even though I dull-headedly understood all this, I jabbered away.

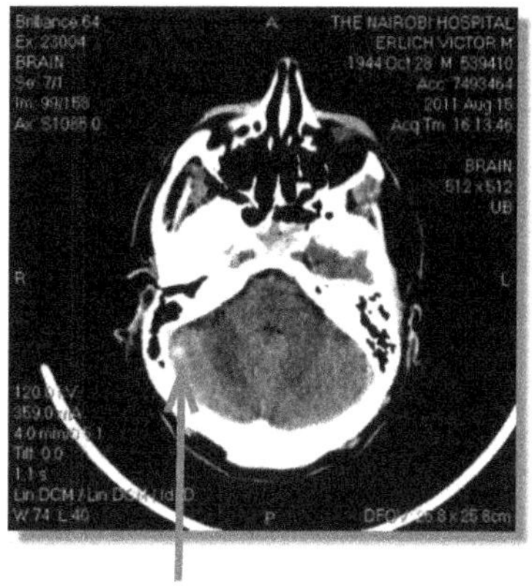

Was damage to my cerebellum making my verbalizations so unkempt? Was there also microscopic injury to my prefrontal cortex, where the tracks from my cerebellum terminated? Was I still drunk on my diminishing doses of opiates?

Elkhonon Goldberg, to whose marvelous book *The Executive Brain* I will soon return, describes several syndromes that can occur after injury to the frontal lobes, one of which is orbitofrontal syndrome, which is caused by injury to that part of the frontal lobes just above the eyeballs. This condition features the inability to restrain oneself from repeating socially inappropriate behavior, which cannot be overridden by judgment. Males, particularly those with injury to the right frontal lobe, are particularly vulnerable to this syndrome, while females, according to Goldberg's studies, possess a more mature ability to overrule urges to respond abruptly and unthinkingly. They are able to brush aside stimuli coming from the current context, to bring to bear their context-independent decision-making, thus avoiding the urge to shoot from the hip. They can restrain themselves. Might I, as a male with an injury to my right frontal lobe, be constantly repeating myself, unable to heed warnings to think before popping off? In this kind of case, says Dr. Goldberg, "The untoward traits are caused by the damage to the orbitofrontal regions of the brain and are not under the patient's control."

Or—I asked myself as I considered what a neurologist would call his differential diagnoses, his list of possible diagnoses—was my being knocked down such a toxic experience as to leave me disabled with a post-traumatic anxiety that I would never go back to work?

I was flown out of Kenya during the Arab Spring. My younger daughter, Margaret, flew immediately from a business meeting in Chicago to Nairobi upon receiving an urgent call from Aaron. She accompanied me on my exodus from Africa, crammed into the small medical jet whose toilet had been removed to make room for medical equipment, including a respirator, leaving no room for Aaron. I learned from Aaron that my flight was diverted to Aswan in Egypt on its way to London because the Libyan brute, al-Gaddafi, had closed Libyan airspace.

In Aswan, Margaret begged to use the bathroom in the airfield's police station. At first, she was told that the facilities were exclusively for Islamic men, so she could pee on the tarmac, as her pilots were doing. When she insisted that she could not do this because of modesty and the 115-degree temperature, the police relented. Margaret told me that the bathroom at the Aswan airfield had gorgeous geometric decorations and lovely murals of lush vegetation, nowhere present in the reality of Aswan and certainly not expected by anyone who has taken in the terminal's harshly geometric architecture.

I was oblivious to the art and architecture, too brain injured and drugged. Margaret belatedly divulged to me what the pilots told her in Aswan: "Your father's temperature is 105 degrees. We are not sure he will make it to London, even on the respirator." Margaret added, "They stripped you and covered you with a wet sheet."

Margaret eventually showed me a photo she had taken of me on my flight from Aswan to Corfu, eventually to London. And here I am, cooled down, caught in a composition made of splashes of blue, gray, and orange, with hints of a patient, a pilot, and a helpful attendant. The attendant's gray shoulder is on the left. The thin tube caries IV fluids, and the thick tube carries oxygen. I was not among those relieved to be off the tarmac, for I have no memory of the heat, the flight, or the photographic composition. My nose was then turned up to it all, but once I saw the photo, I did what I have done throughout my life.

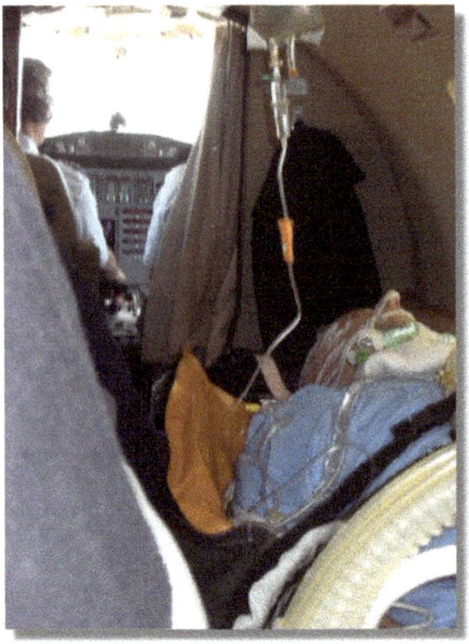

I saw or invented its aesthetic qualities and applied them to the remaking of my life. Margaret's photo reminded me of *Woman with Chin in Hand,* a painting by Richard Diebenkorn, a California artist whose work I first saw in San Francisco when I was a student. The woman is barely recognizable as human—her chin and hand appearing as dinner meat, her torso like that of a dead dog. So disconnected is she, her leg and foot do not seem hers. But the whole is strikingly well executed, beautiful in its own way, a composed jumble of broken space and broken flesh, like me.

Composition, I would learn, is everything. In the artful mind, anything that still has life in it can be composed or recomposed. Artists seem to intuit this, as did Eugène Delacroix, master of many genres of painting. He is famous for his large canvases, like his monumental *Lady Liberty Leading the People*, impressive not only for its scale, but also for its contrasting blend of the black smoke of battle with the voluptuous, towering bare-breasted heroine surrounded by a vivacious burst of white and primary colors. The eye-catching, blood-red flag centers the composition, a semaphore for the creativity that liberty empowers.

The dusky rabble is liberated from their darkness by the golden skirts of sensuality, a fecund impetus for higher, more colorful forces.

Delacroix also produced tiny paintings, such as his *Turkish Slippers,* an oddly chosen subject, worn, sullied, uncoupled, but put together in a lovely way.

Here, Delacroix backs away from the grand and glorious, composing a painting about mindful composition itself, independent of the importance of its subject. He focuses not on a grand and gorgeous dame, but on *babush* (Turkish slippers) in a homely setting. The subject and the setting are one, woven together. The dull background browns and beiges, tinged with a blue glaze, harmonize with the slippers'

faded gold and crimson. Here, composition is more monumental than monuments. The painting is like a still life, a *nature morte,* in Delacroix's French, but it is neither still nor dead, rather quite alive.

After two weeks in a London hospital with sheiks from Arabia, whose Levantine slippers I do not recall, I was loaded onto another, longer medical flight, this time, obliviously home to Seattle.

After I finally mastered the ability to speak coherently, I asked Aaron, "How bad off was I in Nairobi?"

Aaron's basic style is blunt truthfulness.

"You kept making crazy diagnoses of your problems, repetitively. Then later, in London, and again here, you were saying that you had a gynecologic problem. You kept asking about hydrocephalus even when I explained that your doctors said you didn't have that problem. I tried proving it by showing you your CT scans, but that didn't seem to mean anything to you. You had no idea where you were when we were in London, and when we got to Seattle, you thought you were in Detroit. Once we convinced you were in Seattle, you thought that you had driven yourself to the hospital and admitted yourself. You couldn't remember where you'd parked your car, and you didn't believe me when I told you that you hadn't come by car, but had arrived at Harborview via jet and helicopter, and then from the helipad by ambulance. You were in a lot of pain, so the nurses kept giving you oxycodone, and that made you even crazier. We asked them not to give you any more, but they gave it to you anyway. When the drugs made you constipated, you said, 'This is a job for my friend Larry Dabney.' None of us knew what you thought he could do for you, but we laughed about it . . . kind of."

Of course, Aaron could not grasp what I myself could not grasp, that I needed Larry because he was the strongest man I knew, a former soldier in Vietnam, the man who was always chosen to carry the company's heaviest machine gun.

My older daughter, Shala, who left her residency in psychiatry at the University of Vermont to help care for me in London, told me when she visited me later in my hospital room in rehab, "It was even worse than what Aaron told you. When you got to London, the nurses thought that your left arm was the problem. We had to explain to them that the damage to your arm was from the time you were injured when you were four, because you did not understand what they were asking you and could not speak for yourself. I wasn't sure you really recognized me. We didn't know whether you would ever tie your own shoes again—assuming that you would survive, which wasn't clear. And when you were at Harborview, you seemed oblivious to the fact that you were half naked when people came to visit you, even though you were awake and seemed to recognize who was there. You were absolutely shameless."

"I have no memory of that," I told her.

"That may be true," she replied, "but when Debbie, your office manager, came to visit you at Harborview, you couldn't figure out who she was. You asked her, 'Exactly what is your function here?' and she burst out crying. You looked puzzled, not understanding why she was in tears."

"And then, when you left Harborview and got to the Brain Injury unit, you spoke Hebrew with the blonde nurse, Julia, a *shiksa*."

"When she heard my friends call me Avi, she spoke Hebrew to me. Her father was a professor from the Midwest somewhere and loved the Jews. He spent three years teaching in Israel, and Julia went to school there. She speaks Hebrew."

"Well, you still didn't make much sense most of the time."

CHAPTER THREE

How We Evaluate a Brain-Injured Patient

Now King David was old *and* stricken in years; and they covered him with clothes, but he gat no heat. Wherefore his servants said unto him, Let there be sought for my lord the King a young virgin: and let her stand before the King, and let her cherish him, and let her lie in his bosom, that my lord the king may get heat.

– King James Bible, 1 Kings 1:1-2

When I awoke in rehab, I could not sit up. I could not stand. I needed to be accompanied to the bathroom. I repeated myself, unconsciously coming close to babbling. I was infantilized, unmanned, a mess, soulless.

My therapists were, of course, not interested in my soul. They had more practical concerns, ones that dealt with my activities of daily living, known in medical idiolect as ADLs. There was plenty to worry about there. What exactly are the important activities of daily living? Like everybody else, I participated in a lot of activities in a day—too many, I thought in medical school, for a short list. But doctors actually do have a short list. In medical school, to keep this list accessible, I borrowed a mnemonic from a classmate: DEATH. Dress, Eat, Ambulate (including getting up from bed and a chair), Toilet, and pay basic attention to Health, including grooming and bathing.

These were the basics. But there were more. A second mnemonic represents the activities that permit independent living: SHAFT. Shopping, Housekeeping, Accounting (paying bills, being financially sound), Food preparation (including medications), the ability to independently use Transportation and the Telephone. All these must be mastered to avoid the shaft.

So how was I doing with the basics when I arrived at UW Rehab? I needed help with dressing (I couldn't put on my own shoes). I couldn't feed myself—not at first, but I could once I was awake. I could not stand, let alone ambulate, though I could sit up in bed. I needed to be taken to the toilet and have the quantity of my urine measured. I could brush my own teeth and shave with an electric razor that Aaron brought me, though I left patches of stubble. DEATH was not good. SHAFT was worse than its name. I could use the telephone, but only for short spurts. Even my verbosity failed to keep a conversation going. Worse, I was loquacious when I wasn't on the phone.

Whatever the exact cause of my dis-coordinated executive function, I was unable to reassemble my manhood. To re-craft myself was the challenge, but I was too devastated to know this consciously, certainly unable to formulate a plan to attack my problem. Nevertheless, my mind, with its innate plasticity, went to work artfully picking up the pieces of my history and weaving together previous accidents and escapes.

CHAPTER FOUR

Neurology and the Art of the Brain

Herr Settembrini . . . assured them that the world, after passing through a period of inhuman reaction, would always return to the normal order of things. But Herr Naphta preferred to discredit art sooner than admit that it might have a humanizing effect on a sunken wretch.

– Thomas Mann, *The Magic Mountain*

FREUD, WHO BEGAN HIS CAREER AS A NEUROLOGIST, INVENTED psychoanalysis to address a range of rich mental phenomena not explained by the neurology of his day. A hundred years later, Dr. Oliver Sacks also saw modern neurology as inadequate to address—let alone integrate—the full range of human experience and its disruption. Yes, one neuron is connected to another, and yes, the brain talks to itself in order to fuse, in a mysterious way, an image of a rose with the word *rose*. Then the brain connects, through yet another set of neurons, the word *rose* with its fine aroma and its romantic connotations. The neuroanatomists' maps of connectivity are silent about the weaving together of the multiple aspects of infatuation growing into love. The mere assertion that love is driven by that moderator of emotion deep in the limbic brain cannot satisfy, for our deepest feelings do not self-evidently lie in the connectivity of any skein of neurons, which, in any case, do not work like a simple doorbell.

Every time the doorbell is pushed, it chimes exactly the same tune, but our infatuations do not work that way. In the very beginning of *Romeo and Juliet*, William Shakespeare has Romeo sigh a lover's plaint, not about Juliet, whom he has not yet met, but about his current crush, Rosaline, "rich in beauty":

> She'll not be hit
> With Cupid's arrow. She hath Dian's wit.
> And, in strong proof of chastity well arm'd,
> From Love's weak, childish bow she lives uncharm'd.

But the giddy Romeo, adorned with circuitry richer than a doorbell, is soon in Juliet's home—his mind, suddenly reconfigured.

Doorbell circuitry as a basis of human thought and feeling has failed, says Dr. Israel Rosenfield. In his short but marvelous book, *The Strange, Familiar, and Forgotten: An Anatomy of Consciousness*, he asserts that the history of neurology itself demonstrates the "bankruptcy of classical neurology." He accepts that even Jean-Martin Charcot, the founder of modern neurology and the teacher of Freud, was forced to draw diagrams, as was Freud himself, *faute de mieux.* Modern neurology still resorts to wiring diagrams in a desperate attempt to replace the throbbing but slippery and nonscientific psychodynamics of Freud.

"Now is the time," says Dr. Sacks, "to go back to Freud's studies of his patients' living, dynamic minds, to recall them, reuse them, so that there may arise, in our own time, a new and beautiful existential science and therapy." The human mind and its injuries simply cannot be captured by a wiring diagram on the model of an electrician's work order.

Never mind that Freud was something of a fraud, as convincingly laid out by Professor Frederick Crews, who supervised my psychoanalytic study of *Hamlet,* in which I actually disagreed with Freud's interpretation of the play. Crews' derogatory, well-argued opinion of the famous psychoanalyst, as set forth in *Freud: The Making of an Illusion*, goes beyond being a mere disagreement with Freud's many admirers. According to Crews, Freud is naught but a conniving crackpot. But Freud's *The Interpretation of Dreams* still stands as a masterful portrayal of the music of the mind, be it ethereal or cacophonous. Freud began his career as a neurologist, and it may be that his analysis of the mind as a poetic instrument will be his legacy, his therapeutics having fallen largely into disuse.

However psychologically disturbed Freud might have been, some form of psychotherapeutics might have helped him, even if psychoanalysis was the wrong choice. In any case, I submit that the artful appeal to the brain's plasticity gives both the therapist and the patient the power to heal. This requires an effort to marshal a mental poetry that can help rewire the brain and thus remake the man. The artful brain revives itself, as long as it has not been shot to hell. The human brain acts artfully in health and illness, and that's why we study, and must continue to study, art history as part of the humanities.

Among those who have had their artful minds shattered, there are also intermediate cases, between Oliver Sacks and Bauby, as we learn from the famous story of Lev Zazetsky, the brilliant Russian student into whose brain a bullet exploded during World War II. A. R. Luria, along with Zazetsky himself as coauthor, weave the tale in *The Man with a Shattered World*. Dr. Luria urged his patient to try this treatment: "What if he wrote his own story about a terrible brain injury, described his handicaps and his past and present life, to formulate and render coherent the problems a man faces when his world suddenly disintegrates." Zazetsky pursued Dr. Luria's challenge obsessively. For thirty years he tried to rewire his brain by writing his story, writing and rewriting, making painfully slow progress as he revised the same material again and again. But he never returned to the promise of his polytechnic-college days, from which he was drafted to charge into Nazi gunfire.

The accidental, even if it be disastrous, can bring its own blessings if the victim survives long enough to untether his creativity. I was fortunate not to be as badly injured as Zazetsky or Bauby, fortunate to have steeped my mind in a lifetime of reading, drawing, and writing (these were once respectfully called the liberal arts, the foundation of the capacity to live as a free and creative citizen), thus enabling me to shape the vignettes that were most useful to my recovery. I have visited many museums, including the converted home of Louis Pasteur in Paris, where I encountered one of his famous aphorisms, "Chance favors only the prepared mind."

CHAPTER FIVE

Remolding the Brain's Executive Function Requires Failure

There is therefore no deformity but in monstrosity, wherein notwithstanding there is a kind of beauty, Nature so ingeniously contriving the irregular parts, as they become sometimes more remarkable than the principal fabric.

– Sir Thomas Browne, *Religio Medici*, book 1, section 16, 1643

WILLIAM SHAKESPEARE ANTICIPATED MODERN PSYCHOLOGY BY THREE hundred years, becoming the unsurpassed authority on the drama of the mind's struggle to field its creativity against the daily onslaught of conflicting demands, battles that the mind sometimes wins (these are his comedies) and sometimes loses (these are his tragedies). In modern neurology, we speak of the executive function, the brain's orchestral conductor residing in the mid parts of the frontal lobes, the circuitry that harmonizes the totality of the living mind's history, both the well-shaped hopes and the primitive drives, one's experience of the world, one's plans, one's fears, and one's dreams. The executive process produces ethereal music or cacophony, beauty or terror, rational designs or dangerous delusions, each with its own joyful harmony or giddy disharmony. Thus in colloquial speech we use stock phrases, such as "Get a grip on yourself," or "She has put her life in order," or "He's a mess."

I have come to believe that the mind's executive function is Shakespeare's chief subject throughout his career. At least, this seems so from the perspective of a neurologist whose executive function was shattered in the dust of Africa. An intact executive function allows a man to be a man. "I dare do all that may become a man; Who dares do more is none," says Macbeth. He then proceeds precisely to do "more," thus unmanning himself, his executive function disharmonized, a witch's brew, personified by the witches who appear to him.

Though some readers think that Shakespeare meant the witches to be taken literally, this is unlikely, given that Shakespeare rarely is interested in mere literalism. Thus these witches are likely intended to be taken as projections from Macbeth's discomposed mind, full of toil and trouble, as a spell cast upon himself: "Double, double, toil and trouble." The trouble originates in the man's mind and then doubles back on his own head.

Dr. Elchanan Goldberg translates what Shakespeare dramatizes, and other artists have illustrated, into modern neuroscience. He notes that "in *The Creation of Adam*, Michelangelo's great fresco on the ceiling of the Sistine Chapel, God's mantle has the distinct shape of the outline of the brain . . . God's finger, pointed toward Adam and making him human, projects from the prefrontal cortex," the very seat of executive function. Says Dr. Goldberg, "The frontal lobes are truly 'the organ of civilization.'"

Perhaps Michelangelo did not consciously intend his fresco to allude to the brain, but he did know anatomy, having received permission from the papacy to circumvent the ecclesiastical prohibition against mutilating the dead, an old prohibition that came from the Jews. Michelangelo dissected the discarded corpses of vagabonds. Whether or not he looked carefully at human brains, there, in the Sistine Chapel, the fusion of art and neuroanatomy suggests itself: God thrusts His right arm along the cingulate gyrus, part of the brain's control of emotion, thus infusing Adam with "soul" with a single finger, says Dr. Goldberg.

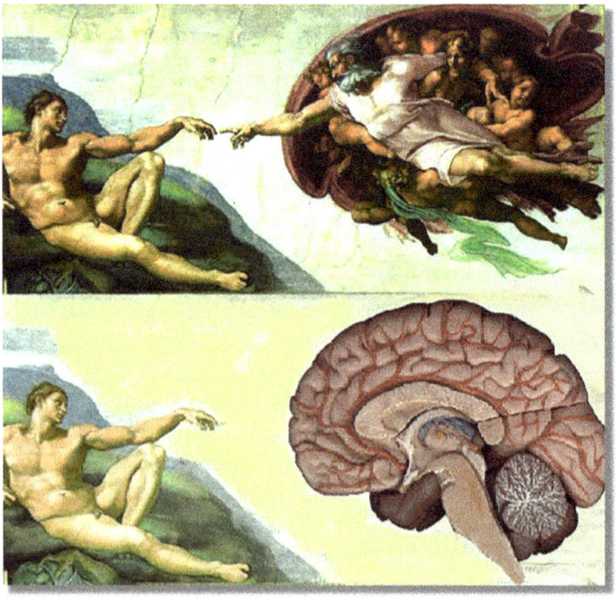

I impatiently awaited the return of my soul, the restoration of my executive function, the harmonization of my befuddled cognitive ability and my frustrated limbic drives.

My injuries can indeed be localized to the mid-portions of the frontal lobes, called by anatomists the mesial frontal lobes, which provide part of the Papez circuit, that part of the human brain that composes our emotional life. The Papez circuit drives the limbic system. It is the incarnation of what some call the human soul.

The mind is indeed divided, with a cognitive function and a limbic function, a division that Freud roughly described as the ego and the id. In more modern neurology, we refer to the neocortex, with its cognitive capacity, which is to be distinguished from the more primitive limbic cortex, with its passions and drives, as pointed out by Michelangelo's rendition of God's left arm and the limbs of His attending angels, which pass through the Papez circuit. The wiring of the limbic system is best viewed in a modern rendition:

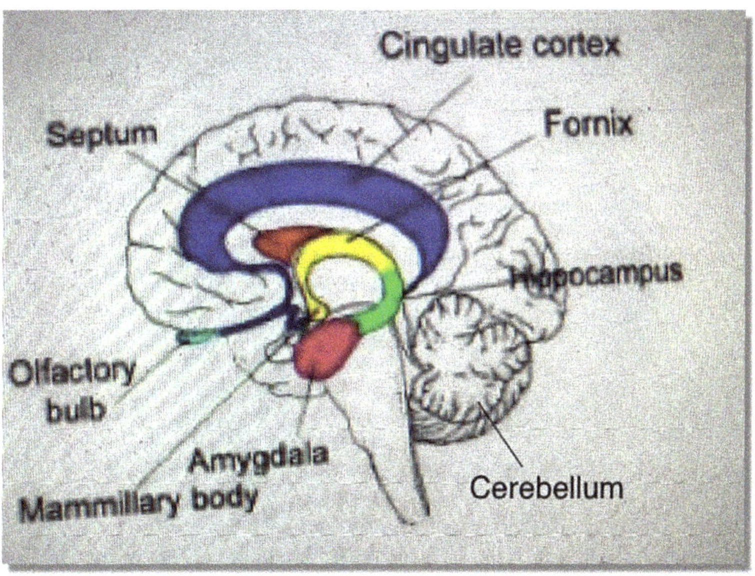

Starting from birth, cells in the amygdala become trained to respond to pleasure and pain. What is recorded in that nucleus of cells can and does last a lifetime, determining preferences and style, choices and compulsions, all often independent of the cognitive centers of the brain, which are located elsewhere. The old saying that there is no accounting for taste is not quite true. There is an accounting. But it is not a cognitive accounting. Taste, style, and preference are limbic drives, not cognitive decisions. The accounting of taste is a story of how and why the limbic system drives one to feel this way or that, of how one's passions are wired, of how one lives and loves, of how one chooses. And there I was, with both limbic and cognitive systems ajar—the pieces there, but now decomposed. I knew that I was in for a long course of rehabilitation.

As I lay in rehab, I was eventually able to reread Ernest Jones' *Hamlet and Oedipus*, brought to me in the hospital by my daughter Shala, who was training to be a psychiatrist. I was glad to have this book in hand, an old friend, first studied when I was young and promising, a graduate student in the English department at Berkeley.

I mulled over *Hamlet*. My memory listened in as Hamlet's executive function worked on a smoothly disguised plot to kill him. The treacherous new king, his stepfather, who murdered his father and bedded his mother, makes a seemingly sporting offer. Claudius, the "bloat king," has devised a stratagem to achieve Hamlet's death "by chance," so "even his mother shall . . . call it accident." Claudius knows nothing about turning accident into art, only how to turn "accident" into mischief. He sweet-talks Laertes, a man who is fuming about Hamlet's killing of his father and sister, into challenging the prince to a duel of rapiers. The planned accident requires the surreptitious poisoning of Laertes' rapier so that "in a pass of practice" (i.e., with a cunning thrust), the prince will perish. Should this "shuffling" fail, Claudius has a backup plan. He will prepare for Hamlet, who will certainly be thirsty, a beverage tainted with a poisoned pearl, "where on but sipping, / If he by chance escape your venomed stuck, / O our purpose may hold."

Hamlet is no dummy, and his executive function immediately integrates multiple mental files. He intuits that danger is afoot. He says to his friend Horatio, "Thou wouldst not think how ill all's her about my heart. But it is no matter . . . We defy augury. There's a special providence in the fall of a sparrow. If it be now, 'tis not to come. If it be not to come, it will be now. If it be not now, yet it will come."

These are not, as is often assumed, merely the despondent words of a man in Hamlet's desperate situation, a student home from university who is now cornered, forced to brood on religion and philosophy as he faces death. Rather, Hamlet's words are a portrayal of the human tragedy of having to carry on when the mind's executive function is overwhelmed. The chiming, alliterative notes heard serially, the pointed rapier, the poisoned pearl, the providential sparrow, help compose Shakespeare's symphony on Hamlet's musical march to his own decomposition. As the prince of Denmark, the heir of his father, he *is* the state of Denmark, and the state of his mind is what is "rotten in the state of Denmark." The "special providence" of which Hamlet speaks emanates not from the god of sparrows but from his own mind. That is what makes it *special.*

Shakespeare's poetry integrates into a single vision the overwhelming demands made on Hamlet's chivalric self, on his cognitive understanding, on his murderous fury, and on his masochistic hatred of his feeble response to his rotten fate. Early on, he chastises himself, "O, what a rogue and peasant slave am I!" And he chimes, "This is most brave, / That I, the son of a dear father murthered, / Prompted to my revenge by heaven and hell, / Must like a whore unpack my heart with words." His chiming, alliterating words, *heaven, hell, whore, heart*, ring out the rack and ruin of a royal mind, his executive function cornered, crippled, unmanned like a whore, rotten. Freud never got the idea of the superego right, though Shakespeare could have helped him here too. The superego is not merely Freud's overweening moral force of guilt; rather it is the frontal lobe's capacity to harmonize limbic and cognitive claims and thus try to escape from a rotten fate like that of Hamlet by achieving a triumphant harmony.

It was a long time before I could make poetry of my recent plight. In fact, my failures were actually necessary. The brain will draw on its capacity to remodel its neuronal wiring only after a current effort, based on current wiring, is unsuccessful. This cerebral plasticity is true of children learning to walk and patients recovering from a stroke. Without my being aware of the specific goal of rewiring myself, I became unusually verbose, beyond my lifelong loquacity, trying again and again to state my plight and thereby right it. Something was rotten in my state, and I kept trying to master it. This repetitive harping alarmed my friends, family, and caregivers, but it was necessary, for failure notifies the plastic brain that a new way of problem solving must be created. Each failure presents an opportunity, demands improvement *ad seriatim* until success is achieved. The healing brain dictates, "If at first you don't succeed, try, try again."

I had to find the art of medicine that would reawaken my brain's music-making, re-orchestrate my accidents so that the ugliness of the individual components was tempered, like the music of Stravinsky and the plays of Shakespeare, like the incense of the ancient Hebrews—that blend of sweet and bitter, frankincense and galbanum.

I am sharing some of my earliest history because it illustrates the kind of material any patient might draw on as part of his or her recovery from brain injury. Until I fell off my bike in Kenya, I had missed only two half-days of work in thirty-seven years. Yet I have suffered much in the realm of physical and emotional trauma, a great deal of it long ago. Much of it was on my mind during my recovery, helping to make that recovery possible. I never quite grasped how much of a patient's past history animates and shapes his or her current predicament, nor did it occur to me that old memories can be woven into one's recovery from a recent accident. To paraphrase William Faulkner, one's past is never dead; it is not even past.

In fact, though a neurologist, I never understood how brain recovery works. When I was a resident in neurology, I learned that after a stroke, one made all the recovery that was possible during the next six months. Then a professor of Latin and Greek at Harvard suffered a stroke, paralyzed on her right side, unable to speak in any language. She reacquired English in one year, Latin in two years, and Greek in three years. The professor published her recovery in the journal *Neurology*, jolting neurologists into the new field of the brain's plasticity.

Though aware of this professor's paper, I never thought about my own brain's plasticity, despite my having used it to master a multitude of accidents. In rehab, I knew from experience that I would have to go back to my art, wherever it might be in my brain.

CHAPTER SIX

The Brain Injury Unit

Disease was the most basic ground
Of my creative urge and stress;
Creating, I could convalesce,
Creating, I again grew sound.

– Heinrich Heine,
"Schöpfungslieder" ("Creation Song")s, c. 1850

On September 15, 2011, I was transferred from the University of Washington Trauma Center at Harborview Hospital to Eight East at the UW Medical Center, the rehabilitation service for the brain injured, where I was supposed to go to work putting my body and mind back together. But on arrival I had no idea where I was or *why* I was wherever I was.

Before I was fully awake, my artful mind concocted a jumbled story from scraps, for injured brains compose as best they can. A woman was asking me questions whose pertinence I could not fathom. I reasoned that this kind, professional-sounding person must be a nurse—so I must be in a hospital. I asked her name.

"Pam."

"Pam, where are you from?"

"Michigan."

From this, I determined that I must have gone to Detroit for a medical conference (something I never would have considered doing), gotten sick there with some gastrointestinal problem, and been taken to hospital, for my main issue at the moment was pain deep in my bowels. I felt badly constipated, but I figured the problem must be much worse than that to have put me in the hospital. I determined that I was now in an auxiliary room of a converted mansion, one of four grand old houses that were on the front lawn of the main hospital, whatever its name, deep in the heart of Detroit. The mansions had been acquired, I guessed, to meet the hospital's chronic problem of overcrowding, and so I was where I was because the main hospital was full.

In a state of confusion, I ran through the possible diagnoses that could explain an acute abdomen. My vague memories from my internship in internal medicine at Montefiore Medical Center in the Bronx got me stuck in the gynecologic branch of the differential diagnoses. Then, suffering from increasing pain, I rang my call button, half delirious. A West African man promptly came in, smiling. I asked him his name.

He said, "I'm Addy. I'm your Constant Observer."

"What's that?"

"I'm here for you all night. The other night, you fell out of bed. Somehow you got over the side rails. Your doctors are worried. You're a fall risk."

I did remember rolling out of bed sometime in the recent past, perhaps even the night before, for all nights were one. I was unable to find a comfortable position. My back and pelvis were aching to the point of desperation, and I was twisting and turning as best as I could, until there was no bed. I was on the floor, no better and no worse. I couldn't and still can't recall how I eventually got helped back under the tormenting covers.

"Addy, can you call Pam for me? I'm terribly constipated, or worse."

"She's taking care of other patients. She'll be with you as soon as she can."

I pictured Michigan Pam in one of the three adjoining auxiliary mansions. Why I decided there were *four* mansions is still a mystery to me, as is my thinking that someone from Michigan must still be in Michigan.

"Please let her know that I need her soon."

Pam, mysteriously and rapidly finding her way back to my mansion, said, as if concluding a simple conversation with me, "I couldn't complete the disimpaction. We'll have to try something else. This pill will help you sleep. It's 2:00 a.m. We'll have something better in the morning."

That entire night I could not escape the deep aching pain in my back and pelvis. I summoned Addy multiple times to turn me, with little benefit. Terminally frustrated, Addy hectored me as if I were a recalcitrant child.

"I just turned you to this position, and now you want to go back to the position from which I just turned you. Your problem is you don't know how to sleep. If you close your eyes, you will fall asleep."

Somehow, in a part of my mind that was still working, I concluded that I was overdosed on opiates, which I had not taken since my hospitalizations in childhood. I asked how much morphine I was being given. The quantity frightened me. I still recall the panic, not the dosage. Every morning, I asked for my morphine to be lowered, a request that did not seem to displease anyone. I knew that many hospitalized patients, in Detroit and Seattle alike, connive to increase pain meds, consequences be damned.

With less morphine, I became less foggy and less constipated, but, apparently, no less brain injured, according to the experts. Brain injured or not, I now realized I needed a bath, and, by chance, at that moment in walked Julia, the blonde nurse from the Midwest who spoke Hebrew.

"Have you had a bath recently?" she asked innocently.

"I didn't know that you had baths here."

"I'll get Addy to wheel you into the shower and put you on a shower bench."

Within minutes, Addy lifted me like a feather out of my wheelchair onto the hard, plastic shower bench with a sturdy back. I thanked him.

"It was nothing. You weigh only 141 pounds."

"I weighed 168 pounds when I left for Africa."

"We have plenty of food here."

CHAPTER

SEVEN

Prior Accidents and Hospitalizations

We see it is accounted an error to commit a natural body to empiric physicians, which commonly have a few pleasing receipts [prescriptions] whereupon they are confident and adventurous, but know neither the causes of diseases, nor the complexions of patients, nor peril of accidents [symptoms], nor the true method of cures.

– Sir Francis Bacon, *The Advancement of Learning*, 1605

WHILE UNDERGOING REHABILITATION, I COULD NOT BUT BE REMINDED of other hospitalizations, for I had never recovered from my tonsillectomy or my being run over by a milk truck, both so deeply inscribed in my hardy limbic system, so still present in my mind while in rehab in 2011. The early assault on my throat at age three colored my response to further trauma, especially when I yet again had a foreign body shoved down my throat at age sixty-six—intubated in Kenya, still on a ventilator in London and even in Seattle, on a breathing machine all together for thirty days. Yes, memories of old trauma produce anxiety, but they also can be woven into recovery from new trauma.

A taxi arrived early one morning when I was three years old. This was unusual. My mother was making slow progress as a new driver, and Uncle Shesh, her younger brother, already a Jewish chaplain in the US Army at the age of twenty-one, was having a hard time teaching her. She was still not driving with any passengers, so if I went anywhere with my mother, it had to be within walking distance: out to Lincoln Boulevard, but not any farther. Uncle Shesh said that my mother was frightened of traffic, even on quiet streets, and on busy streets, she was afraid to turn left until there was no oncoming traffic in sight. Sometimes she made a series of right turns around a block to avoid a left turn. Uncle Shesh always liked to have a cup of coffee with sugar before the lesson.

On his last visit, I took advantage of the opportunity to run an experiment to answer a question that was bothering me. Since sugar looked like salt, I wasn't sure whether they were truly different substances or became what they were by being put in either the saltshaker or the sugar bowl. So while my mother was making coffee for Shesh, I switched the contents of the saltshaker and the sugar bowl, both on the dining room table. I then waited to see what would happen. Shesh spit it out and spluttered, "Mary, what did you put in this coffee?"

You might wonder why the daughter of the chief Orthodox rabbi of Los Angeles was called Mary. When my mother went to kindergarten in Winnipeg, Canada—where her father was able to get a pulpit after he fled the Russian Communists who had taken over his town of Mezhirich, near Kiev in The Ukraine—she was one of a number of Jewish girls in her class whose names all started with the letter M: Malka (three of these), Miriam (two), and Michal (one). My mother's name was Michlah. The school called all seven of them *Mary,* not out of disrespect, but to honor them, for Mary was the name of God's mother.

In any case, on one particular morning when Uncle Shesh was unavailable, a taxi arrived at our home. But why had we not had any breakfast? My mother told me that we were going to buy toys, but we never took a taxi to buy toys. I knew she was lying, but I couldn't figure out why. It had something to do with her sadness, with the fact that her mother had died when she was only four and Uncle Shesh was eighteen months.

The taxi driver dropped us in front of a large building. There, we walked through basement corridors filled with bins of laundry. There were no windows. I was surprised to see a barbershop down there with the same red- and white-striped pole I'd seen in front of barbershops on the street.

A man with purple splotches on his face was getting a haircut. On his forehead was a large white knob, stark against his purple face. I remember him vividly today—though he's been dead these many decades—deformed by a knob and spruced up by a haircut, on this occasion, the aesthetics of grooming failing to overcome monstrosity.

As we walked along, my mother told me we were not going to buy toys—at least, not at the moment. I had to have my tonsils out first, the part of me at the back of the throat that was making me sick. But since I didn't feel sick, I suspected this could be another lie, though it sounded like the truth.

After we took an elevator out of the basement, run as usual by an elevator man, the nurses told me that parents couldn't stay. They had to visit during visiting hours. I knew that if I were going to be hurt, my mother wouldn't have walked away calmly. The nurses would have had to drag her away. She trusted the *shiksas*, so they must be OK.

My clothes were confiscated, and I was given a gown that was open in the back, like an unfinished dress. I couldn't keep myself covered as I was wheeled about on a narrow bed made of shiny steel into a room where everybody was wearing masks. They stood around a steel table upon which I was placed. The lights surrounding me were set in half melons of polished steel. The people in the masks were silent until one of them announced, "This will make you go to sleep."

I was then tied up. The bright surgical lights blinded me, and the stench of a gas choked me. They sloshed a towel filled with more stench over my face, smothering me. I later learned the name of the stench, *ether.*

When I awoke, I saw my mother and father. They tried to cheer me up by offering me ice cream, but with my throat on fire, the cold ice cream made it burn even more. Despite my confusion about ice cream feeling hot, and my outrage about being tricked into trading toys for ether, I dimly realized they meant me no harm. And now in rehab, I was dimly coming to new realizations.

The smothering ether and the surgical lamps became objective correlatives of betrayal and fear. Surgical lamps are much like the lights in dental offices, and the latter still make me quake. By this point it had become clear to me that it was better to be the man with the scalpel, or even the man with the stinking towel, than it was to be the boy getting the tonsillectomy. I would be the doctor, not the patient, I decided. Then, recalling my name, I made a slight revision: I would be the victor, not the victim.

After my tonsillectomy, I didn't eat much, but I had hateful crumbs in my bed anyway. My father was good at cupping them out with his hand, but my mother didn't know how to do it. To this day, breakfast in bed is a torment—and even worse if it's being served to me in the hospital.

Uncle Shesh came to visit me in the hospital. Tan and oddly happy, he brought me a squirt gun.

"Use it at the beach," he told me. "But be careful. The salt water might gum up the mechanism."

"What's a mechanism?"

"It's the pump that shoots. But if you put salt water in the squirt gun now and shoot it into your mouth and gargle, it will make your throat feel better." And then he squirted me.

When I told him he was right, he smiled. And because he was happy, my mother smiled; she couldn't help it. But her smile did not reassure me. It put ice in my veins. Even Uncle Shesh's explanation of the word *mechanism* was but a small comfort.

After I left the hospital, my tonsils safely out, the ice in my veins begot pyromania. I liked the faint sulfurous smell of a box of wooden matches that my mother kept next to the stove to light the pilot light, which was always going out. I liked the feel of the box in my hand, the rattle of the matches, the delicacy of the wooden shaft, which fractured if I struck too hard. I liked the potency of the yellow flame flickering up, the jump of its odor, its sudden birth—the blue center of the flame surrounded by a bright yellow-orange that settled down to yellow. I liked to let the fire burn toward my fingers, the wood curling as I blew out the flame just in time.

I took the box of matches out to our back alley, up against the open fields of the working farm there. A man was plowing way over by Marine Street. I got old newspapers together and lit them, staring at the magical flames. I was stamping out the fire when the man on the tractor startled me. Since I am deaf in my left ear, I hadn't heard his tractor. I stared at the fire, too stupid to survive.

"What are you doing, son?"

He was a short man with pink skin and a baseball cap. He didn't wear overalls like the farmers in books. Rather, he was dressed like my father, in khaki trousers and a matching work shirt. White hair stuck out of the top of his shirt to his neck, as if he were a turkey. Little red veins covered the tip of his nose. I later learned that this was a sign he drank too much alcohol. He turned off the tractor and climbed down.

"Hey, lookee over there. Do you see the fox?"

I looked where he pointed and saw a red dog sitting quietly.

"You won't see them foxes around here much longer. There won't be any farms here either, just houses and streets. And maybe a golf course at the end of Commonwealth, where the abandoned farm is, which is still good for tramps and foxes. Foxes don't like golf courses. And if you keep lighting fires, there won't be any houses either, and then the foxes will come back. Be careful."

After learning this, I was afraid to light fires behind our house again. I went across Commonwealth to the alley between Lynn's house and Dickie's house on Warren Street and lit fires there. I found old newspapers, made small fires, and stamped them out. I didn't light near anything that could burn. I liked the control over the crackle, and I liked the shriveling of the blackened paper before I crushed it into ashes under my shoe.

But I didn't know how to be careful. One day I lost control of a fire in Dickie's alley. Somehow, a trashcan caught fire, along with the fence behind it. It couldn't have been my fault because I was always careful to stay away from the trashcans and fences, but nevertheless, a trashcan and a redwood fence were on fire. I ran away: down the alley alongside Lynn's garage, which his father had fixed up to look like the inside of a submarine, and then safely across Commonwealth Avenue.

Soon I heard sirens. Two firemen were suddenly in our living room with my mother. One fireman spoke softly. He wore a black raincoat and rain pants, black boots, and a black hat with a badge in front. I kept my eyes on his black boots, which were still wet, like the boots Houston wore at my father's kosher slaughtering plant, except Houston's boots displayed feathers stuck to chicken blood. The fireman's boots were clean.

He tried to be nice. He spoke on and on, but he never asked me if I was the one who set the fire. He already knew. How he knew was a mystery. Nobody could have seen me. I didn't form a memory of what he said, though I still have vivid memories of trying and failing to reconstruct his words.

After the firemen left, my mother spoke. To this day I recall her desperately kind tone. She was frightened there was something about me that would take me away from her.

"They had to spray a lot of water. You will go to jail and eat nothing but dry bread and water."

I had heard that before.

What occurs before becomes part of what occurs afterward, and what occurs afterward is woven into a new tapestry. Thus my tonsillectomy is woven into my story about being run over by a milk truck when I was four, and both stories intertwine with the hypothetical wildebeest in Kenya. Did not James Joyce say in *A Portrait of the Artist as a Young Man*, "I am tomorrow, or some future day, what I establish today. I am today what I established yesterday or some previous day"? Is there not a portrait of a young man in a brain-injured old man?

When my father came home from the war, we got an icebox for our little house on Commonwealth, like the neighbors. The ice slowly melted and had to be replaced, so an ice truck came regularly. With tongs, the driver swung a block of ice up to his shoulder. He protected his back with a leather cape and struggled up the cement steps at the back of our house. My mother, fine-boned, petite, delicately made but anxious, held open the screen door. The sharp points of the man's tongs bit into the ice. We kept our icebox near the backdoor for him.

Other trucks also came down our dead-end street. A Good Humor ice-cream truck drove by regularly, tempting me on one occasion to buy an ice pop with my twenty-five-cent weekly allowance, which I was supposed to save for college and medical school. My ice-cream purchases disappointed my mother, but then she allowed me to buy a weekly doughnut from the Helms Bakery truck for ten cents. I didn't like the jelly doughnuts because they were sloppy, but that was OK because they cost more. UPS trucks came too, and they terrified me because I could not penetrate the mystery of their function. And, of course, a Carnation Milk truck delivered milk daily in glass bottles.

On July 19, 1949, I was run over by a Carnation Milk truck three months before I turned five. The vivid memories of this accident shadowed me throughout my life, but it was not until I was in rehab that I realized that all my patients were likely haunted by memories of past trauma. My particular memories of that milk truck and its consequences were raised out of a quiet background to serve my recovery from my bicycle crash in Africa.

Our neighbor across the street, Lynn's father, had built a replica of the submarine on which he'd served in the Pacific. He also kept an army surplus motorcycle with a sidecar parked at the curb. Sometimes, my mother told me, Lynn's father slept in his submarine because it reminded him of the good times he had during the war. My father hated him because of the submarine and the motorcycle. When I was four-and-a-half years old, my mother allowed me to cross the street to play on the motorcycle. It was the genuine article.

I knew my father had been "in the field," in the Battle of the Bulge, so it was natural that I liked playing war games with the other children in the bean field past the end of our street. In the deep weeds, we chased Imaginary Japanese soldiers, causing vice butterflies to spring up in profusion, like moths.

One Sunday in July, my father was again preparing to take our family to Venice Beach, less than a mile away. While my mother was packing a picnic, I crossed Commonwealth to join kids who were playing on the motorcycle. Lynn, who wore one chartreuse sock and one hot-pink sock, gave orders, shouting: "Gun 'em! Gun 'em down! What's wrong with you?"

As my father loaded the trunk of our '46 Chevy, he ignored the kids playing on the motorcycle, because he hated the thing. I sat in the sidecar, the coveted spot, while the other kids hung on to the gunwales. The enemy crouched in the weeds, and I stared them down, not shooting. The morning sun was hot, and heat haze warped my view of the bean field. Lynn gave me hell for doing nothing.

My father came back out of the house with another load, wearing his faded-yellow trunks and carrying a beach blanket over one arm. He held a red metal cooler with a white Coca-Cola label, the letters large and nicely embossed. Inside the cooler, at the center, was a tin container for ice. He called me across the street to get into the car, turning his back to load the cooler.

A Carnation Milk truck was positioned near the Japanese hideout at the dead end, making a quiet delivery to Dirty Audrey's house, the shabbiest on the block, really a shack. In my memory, the milk truck is still safely parked behind a curtain of heat haze over the bean field on that hot July Sunday in 1949. But it wasn't parked. It was moving.

I looked left and right before crossing from the motorcycle to my father, in his faded-yellow trunks. Did I run? I do not know. I have no memory of crossing, just pseudo memories, fantasies from later, when I pictured myself crossing from the motorcycle after making sure that the milk truck was still at the end of the street. Did I dart across the street, right in front of the milk truck, giving the driver no chance to stop? Or was the driver inattentive, negligent? I probably assumed my father had looked to make sure it was safe for me, and then I took off. I was run over, pulled under the chassis, and dragged a hundred feet.

I awoke on my parents' bed. I saw that my left arm was a crush of red meat surrounding an island of perfectly white bone, which stuck out where the elbow used to be. I thought, *This isn't my arm.* I wondered why this mangled thing was being delicately packed in cotton in my presence. Then I felt the soft sensation of the cotton as a surprising relief, and I realized, *It must be my arm.* And now the arm was covered and no longer painful, so all might yet be well.

A man with blond hair was telling me that we were going to the hospital in an ambulance and not to mind the blood. "You were hit by a milk truck, not badly." This blond angel-man made me believe I would be whole again. The cotton was in a roll, with blue backing. He unrolled it under my arm and rolled it up again. My arm disappeared, safe. I can still feel the softness of that cotton on my flayed arm. I can feel how I anesthetized myself, steeled myself with a sham-heroic pretense that disaster did not matter. After all, disaster didn't ruin life for Jesus, as shown in the window of the Christian bookstore on Lincoln Boulevard.

After my arm was wrapped, the blond man applied dressings to my head, where there was a bleeding, hairless spot, then to my knees, my dangling right ear, and my right shoulder. He kept explaining what he was doing, as nice angels do. He paid special attention to my right ear, which had to be rotated up to my skull. I was then carried outside on a gurney to the ambulance. I saw my mother lying face down on our patch of front lawn, pounding the grass.

Even if I couldn't understand a UPS truck, I knew an ambulance, just as I knew a Studebaker with a rocket nose and a Buick with portholes. I was aware that we were going to the hospital, and from my tonsillectomy, I understood what that was.

I underwent surgeries, yet again suffocated into unconsciousness by ether, as the powerful surgical lamps glared at me. There is nothing closer to death than being under the influence of ether. My right ear was reattached to my head. The surgeons tried several times to reset my left elbow, but the joint was crushed. The proximal end of the radius floated free, out of joint, because there was no joint. The elbow would never be able to rotate. I soon learned that my left hand could turn palm down but not palm up, able to grasp a book but unable to turn a cupped palm to receive Uncle Shesh's silver dollar.

A deep gash on my right shoulder was sutured, but it healed with a rope of keloid. A twenty-five-cent-sized abrasion on my upper right scalp would prevent hair from ever growing there again. Multiple skin grafts from my abdomen were harvested for my left elbow and right ear. The surgeons dug so deeply while grafting skin from my left abdomen that more keloids grew there in the shape of Mexico, as it appeared on my puzzle of the United States.

I was confined to the hospital as the summer passed. Nurses changed dressings roughly and woke me nightly to sign me over to the next shift. In my sleep, the lights would sometimes explode, as bright as surgical lamps, as nurses pointed at this part and that part before shutting them off. The nurses didn't meet my eyes, just pointed at my damaged parts, just as Addy did decades later.

Purple ropes of scar compounded the bone deformities of my left elbow. On the top of my right ear, a purple orange began to grow. My right shoulder, where a purple rope lay, looked as if it had been whipped.

I asked my mother, "Will my arm be normal when I'm five?"

"Maybe not by then."

"When I'm six . . . or ten? Or fifteen?"

My mother said, "If God's so wishes. *Eem yirtseh ha-Shem.*"

The boy in the bed kitty-corner from mine was strung up in traction. He had smashed his leg when he fell off a slide at the beach. I had jumped off high slides at Venice Beach and landed safely, so I wondered how he'd sustained so much damage and why he just lay there, never looking out his window, like a zombie. I promised myself that I would again jump harmlessly into the hot sand. Meanwhile I was locked up in my contraption called a hospital, just inland from the beach, up from which a wooden staircase led up to the Santa Monica Pier. I had already practiced jumping off the first stair, then the second, then the third, and finally the last—twenty-two steps above the sun-warm sand.

After a month in that hospital, just within sniffing range of the salty ocean, I left its bewildering routines—the staff shifts, the bursts of light in the middle of the night, the crumbs in the bed. I wanted to walk out of the hospital, but my father carried me to the car. I let him carry me because I figured there must be a rule that requires a damaged child to be carried out of hospital. I don't believe that I was conscious of being angry. I was probably glad that my father was taking me home. But to this day, I also remember a quiet, bitter feeling I had while being carried out of the hospital, for my father had called me to him in his faded-yellow trunks, and I'd been run over. The radioactive phrases, "My father called me" and "I was run over" endured wordlessly in my subconscious.

As my father carried me, I tasted the August air: the salt of the beach mixed with carnations and car exhaust—delicious. I craved splashing in the ocean, braving the shallow breakers, where I was allowed to stand—"not too deep," as my mother would say. To be in the sun again was to escape from damage despite a smashed left elbow, a deaf left ear and a torn one on the right.

My father's father loved me. In an earlier photo with my grandfather, I am holding on to his left hand with my right hand, smiling, reaching out with my left arm gamely, for it was still normal then. Looking at the photograph today, I see how much I now resemble my grandfather, who was sixty-six years old when it was taken, exactly my age when I fell into the dirt of Africa.

Out from under the milk truck, out of the hospital, I became a child apart, in the hope that keeping quiet would make me strong again. The cast still weighed down my left arm, but the enforced extra effort, I thought, was good for me. My right ear looked like broccoli. I took to wearing a baggy purple sweater to cover the cast. My mother found it for me when I asked for long sleeves. It made me hot in the late summer heat of Los Angeles, but I wore it anyway. I knew I was fooling nobody. Everybody knew I'd been run over, that I'd had an "accident," a word that made ice run through my veins.

Wearing my ugly purple sweater, I felt brave enough to cross Commonwealth and cut through Lynn's backyard to Dickie's house on Warren Avenue, where Dickie's father, Frankie, would sometimes station his yellow inflatable war surplus lifeboat in the driveway, facing the garage.

Dickie and his friends took turns running down the drive, leaping over the stern, and landing on the prow, ready for action in the Pacific. The same ocean lay only a mile away, truly pacific, with waves foaming up to the warm sand, whispering about their journey, unlike those on Frankie's beaches of bombardment.

Still wearing a cast covered by the purple sweater, I stood back on the sidewalk, planning my jump in the early September heat. As I ran down the driveway toward the yellow boat, I calculated that the weighty cast required a prodigious leap. Frankie stood to the side, watering the back lawn in his baggy swim trunks—his stomach, a watermelon; his calves, cantaloupes. As I approached him, he yelled, "Give a good jump."

I wanted to reach the soft prow without dropping ignominiously into the hold that lay hard on blacktop. With quietly growing muscles, I sailed over the entire boat, skidding into the garage on my nose, blood streaming. I wiped blood on the bumper of Frankie's new Buick.

Frankie picked me up and carried me into the house. The floor plan was similar to ours, but with nicer furniture and none of my little brother Harvey's pish on the rug. Rosie, Frankie's mother, dabbed the blood off my face. She was easygoing, always happy—not a brooder, like my mother. She had blond hair, and so did Frankie and Dickie. They didn't throw in so many Yiddish phrases when they spoke, and they didn't spit three times when they talked about something they feared might happen. My mother was both smart and scared.

"There," said Rosie. "There wasn't so much blood after all. It just looked like a lot. A drop of blood in the toilet bowl makes the water look beet red. There's just a little skin missing from your nose. It will grow back in no time. Some of the blood must have come from inside your nose, but it's stopped now."

I went back outside. All the other kids had fled except Dickie.

Frankie said, "You're going to be the best jumper in kindergarten."

"Will my nose be healed by then?"

Frankie smiled.

"It will be, but you'll have a black scab."

Dickie came up to me and put his arm around me.

"It was a good jump. I wish I could jump like that."

Two weeks later, Dickie and I entered the new yard of Broadway School's expanded kindergarten on Lincoln Boulevard, each carrying a new lunch pail with the picture of the Cisco Kid on it.

I was terrified when Mrs. Tucker announced there would be hearing tests. I feared that the hearing test would uncover my deaf left ear, with more ether sure to follow.

Luckily, the test started with my right ear. The nice lady told me to raise my right hand every time I heard a tone. During the test of my right ear, I counted the seconds between tones, estimated how long the tones lasted, and memorized the delay between the time I raised my hand and the onset of the next tone. When the test moved to my left ear, I was able to repeat what I had done on my right side, even though I heard nothing. When I thought that I had tested well enough on my left ear, I stopped raising my right hand.

"Fine," said the nice lady. "You're above normal in both ears, but the left is superb."

It was easy to fool her. She was busy testing all the children at the beginning of the first year of the double-sized kindergarten building. This was because of the "baby boom." Later, the experts said the baby boom didn't start until 1946, but I was born in 1944, and when I went to kindergarten, I was told that their building had been doubled in size to accommodate me. Sometimes the experts are wrong about when things happened and what will happen next.

My trick with hearing tests worked in the first grade too, but when I was tested in the third grade, the tester smartened up, arranging the sounds irregularly. I was then sent to Dr. Victor Goodhill, who squirted cold water in my ears. He said that I was deaf on the left, but there was nothing that could be done about it, even if we did share the same first name.

CHAPTER EIGHT

Constipation and Past Medical History

Thus finishing his grand survey,
Disgusted Strephon stole away
Repeating in his amorous fits,
Oh! Celia, Celia, Celia shits!

– Jonathan Swift, "The Lady's Dressing Room"

SUPINE IN REHAB, UNABLE TO STAND, IMMOBILE, AND CONSTIPATED, I found my mind wandering. I recalled my past experiences with patients who suffered from constipation, and drifted into a formal medical History and Physical Examination (H&P) of me as patient. Every patient's H&P, the author's included, begins with a laser focus on the Chief Complaint (CC), goes on to the History of Present Illness (HPI), then progresses to a summary of the Past Medical History (PMH), Medications, Allergies, Family History (FH), Social History (SH), and Review of Systems (ROS—an inquiry into the working of all the patient's organs). I had worked diligently to master this format, which had now become sorrowfully relevant to me.

Most medical students do not see, nor are they taught, the aesthetic nature of the H&P. The parts are like stanzas in a poem. They converge on a theme, the diagnosis, that which is known by seeing through a plethora of surface detail to the unifying idea. The diagnosis is a marvelous work of integration, beautifully woven together, as complex as a Hieronymus Bosch painting, as orchestrated as a Shakespearean sonnet, even as sweet as a sour satire by Jonathan Swift. In the case of a medical poem, the history and physical, and all the other stanzas drawn from laboratory and radiologic data, are but proxies for being able to look directly at the anatomy and physiology of the patient's body, and directly into his or her psychology.

Though I was too confused and despondent to realize that nobody in rehab ever asked me about my past medical history, it is true that nobody did. Three months after I was discharged, Dr. Pepping, while preparing me for my upcoming cognitive testing as an outpatient, asked me nonchalantly, "Did you ever suffer head trauma in the past?" Terrified that I was already in hot water, and knowing that a second head trauma is often more dangerous than the first, I lied, answering "No," suppressing the fact that I had a bald spot on the crown of my head, the result of having been dragged over asphalt by the milk truck.

Nobody on rehab ever asked me about my childhood accidents; about my lame left arm, with its knobby elbow; or about my deaf left ear. Nor was anybody interested in what psychological effects consequent to these accidents might be pertinent now, even though my lameness and left-ear deafness were obvious to anyone who cared to look. Nobody even asked me about my current broken bones, whether I might like to speak to an orthopedist, for the problem of my fractures was already addressed at Harborview Hospital. Probably because I couldn't walk, nobody seemed to realize that my left leg was now an inch shorter than my right. Technically, it wasn't *shorter,* but it was shoved so far up into my pelvis that it behaved as if it were shorter.

And nobody on rehab ever asked me if I had ever before suffered from constipation, though I had. While in the hospital after having been run over by the milk truck, I became severely constipated. The memory of this flooded back into my teeming mind, there in the haze of the ancillary mansion in Detroit. While caged in the hospital after the milk truck incident, kitty-corner from the silent boy strung up in traction, I stopped moving my bowels so the nurses at the foot of my bed couldn't write down my "doodies." I wanted more control. I wouldn't move my bowels unless I absolutely had to.

These childhood memories brought forth images of Hieronymus Bosch's *Garden of Earthly Delights* sinner being swallowed by an avian monster before being defecated into a hellish hole, while a nearby sinner dangles, rectally impaled, shafted. As I myself lay dying in Detroit, in rectal pain and mentally confused, I was also in Los Angeles in 1949, run over and constipated, as well as in Bosch's medieval hell. This kind of conflation of places and times is humorous from a distance, but terrifying if you are there. Yet the injured physician's capability of integrating these fragments in his ruminating mind helped to heal him, as did his composition of fragments of his hospitalization in Santa Monica in 1949, his fabrication of a room in a mansion in Detroit in 2011, and his recollection of Hieronymus Bosch's painting from 1504. My visions, combined with those of Bosch, which are lovely in their orchestration, helped stimulate the plasticity of my brain to weave me back together.

My phantasmagoric thoughts in my Michigan mansion faded into a dream, which, bizarre as it was, did manage to include the realization that I was in Seattle. I dreamt that I was discharged from the hospital in Detroit and arrived home in Seattle, by what means I did not bother to imagine. In my dream, I found myself still in pain at home, drove myself to the University of Washington Hospital, parked my car somewhere, and admitted myself for further care. Somehow, despite my having been transported from Michigan to Washington, Pam was still my nurse, announcing that she would call a specialist about my constipation.

Would it have made a difference to me if a specialist could have figured out that my past medical history was both a well-woven whole and a nightmare affecting me deeply, even then in rehab? Such a specialist, a physician of the mind, might have alleviated my despondency. This physician might have asked me how my treatment might be crafted to best meet my needs. What ideas might I have about how we should proceed was a question never asked. For, after all, what ideas could a brain-injured patient have on this score? I was given the usual protocol, actually a good one, always administered by a caring staff, but not by anyone who was interested in learning my history or what my opinions about rehabilitation might be. I never did endorse the standard protocol. I was given an antidepressant.

I actually knew from my work on stroke patients that a patient's endorsement of the plan for his rehabilitation determines to a large extent its success. If the patient's limbic system doesn't validate the plan, it won't work as well as it would if the patient is convinced that it will. In 2002, a key study along these lines was published in the journal *Stroke* by a team of astute English researchers. It was titled "The Concept of Patient Motivation." I am afraid this concept had escaped me until I needed rehab myself. I'd always plowed forward, assuming that patients would appreciate my earnest efforts. Niall Maclean, the lead author of this study, concludes, "The blurred boundaries of the criteria used to identify motivation mean that patients must strike a delicate balance between proactivity and compliance to avoid being categorized as unmotivated."

And there I was, terrified not only of being categorized as unmotivated but also of being branded as unable to follow the prescribed program because of brain injury. The old professor in me liked keeping my students and myself focused on relevance and coherence, but in rehab, I was driven to repeat my questions to all those who would listen, even to those who didn't care to listen to my rambling repetitions. My caregivers probably did not have a way of knowing that my grit, woven with my interests in art and literature, would obviate their need to motivate me.

I might have been asked to watch videos of the Department of Neurology's Grand Rounds, to which the hospital had access, or I could have asked to write essays on nonmedical subjects, say on Hieronymus Bosch or Kandinsky or Alexander Calder. I could have been asked to write about the poetry of King David, Shakespeare, painting, neurology, or psychoanalysis. Had they thought me capable of discussing these subjects without falling into a tedious verbosity, they might have asked me to write an essay about *Coriolanus*, Shakespeare's most focused study of a character with poor executive function. This approach would have been an improvement over asking me again and again to figure out from clues problems such as this: how might a young mother best schedule her grocery-shopping; collect her dry cleaning; get to her job; and, finally, chauffer her daughter to and from an evening dance lesson?

That every patient is an individual with a rich soul is an old medical truism that I myself have forgotten more times than I care to remember. I learned in medical school that doctors, belonging to a 2,500-year-old calling, were once well educated. They knew Latin and Greek, Homer and Virgil, Shakespeare and the Bible. That they are no longer well educated seems a poor excuse to have largely confined my cognitive therapy to figuring out from appropriate clues the order in which six bicyclists arrived at the beach for a swell day (yes, cyclists did turn up in a word puzzle I was given). You see, the cyclists arrived at the beach ten minutes apart, each having taken different routes. Ed arrived first, with the towels. Joel had the picnic food, arriving twenty minutes after Hal. Barbara went for a swim, without a towel, when she arrived, and was later joined by Sarah. When the girls got out of the water, the towels and food were there, and so was Ann. They all enjoyed themselves, for they did not fear that they might never ride again.

However simple this puzzle might be, I took too long to get the answer. I was slower than the interns, who were becoming cognitive therapists. Figuring out the right order of arrival for the six cyclists debilitated me: Ed, Barbara (somebody had to arrive between Ed and Hal), Hal, Ann, Joel, and Sarah arrived at the beach in that order, but I had overreached when I concluded that I had done well.

“We can help you with this problem,” said my kind therapist.

And this brought forth another memory of overreaching.

CHAPTER NINE

A Fall from the Rafters, Age Eight

Him the Almighty Power,
Hurl'd headlong flaming from th' Ethereal Skie
With hideous ruine and combustion, down
To bottomless perdition.

– John Milton, *Paradise Lost,* book 1, lines 44–47

As a third grader at Castle Heights Elementary School, I walked uphill on Beverly Drive from our new home to Stuart's house to play Ping-Pong, a game I liked because I needed only one good arm.

I said, “We can play war the way real soldiers fought, up in the rafters. We can use the table to get up there.”

Stuart said he could get up on the rafters without the table. He crouched down, swung his arms up as he jumped, just reaching a rafter with his fingertips, and pulled himself up easily. Nobody could jump like that. I got on the table and then up to the rafters with a bit of a jump and a strong pull with my right arm; my left helped out too.

We then proceeded to shoot at each other with our fingers.

“This is stupid,” said Stuart.

I turned to look at him and slipped off my rafter. I caught myself before I fell, but only barely, hanging by my fingers. I was not over the Ping-Pong table, so I tried to slide that way, catching a splinter. The pain made me let go with my left hand. I tried to get another grip, but instead I fell. I wanted to roll as I fell, but I stretched my right hand out to protect myself. I could tell that I broke something. My wrist was already swelling.

I was soon in the emergency room. A technician took me to the x-ray machine. She had a big butt and waddled as she went.

She asked, “Which arm is broken?”

I showed her my right arm.

“Humph,” she said, looking at my misshapen left arm as if that might’ve been my reason for being there.

The doctor came back with films.

“Luckily, it’s a non-displaced fracture at the wrist, quite small, actually. When you’re young, bones bend and crack rather than break. But you’re going to need a cast. Six weeks, and you’ll be as good as new. Do you see the fracture here?”

On the x-ray, the white bones of my forearm and hand floated on a black background. I could see how they all fit together as a system. I was surprised by their number, laid out with nothing holding them together, each finger a train of little bones, ready to go. And the trains were going into a cast.

My mother looked at the x-ray too.

She said, "You have to stop being so accident prone. Do you remember the last time we were in this emergency room? When you leaned back hard on the rocking chair in the den and knocked the standing lamp with the large glass top back into the wall? You shattered the fixture and nearly cut off your nose! You are lucky that it didn't keloid. And the time before that, when you were making that monstrosity you called a sculpture, nailing a bunch of cans together on an orange crate until you hammered your thumb? The bleeding under your nail couldn't get out. We had to take you to the emergency room. The doctor had to drill a hole in your nail, and then you lost your nail, but you could have lost your thumb. And do you remember before that, when you were drawing what you called 'murals' on the back wall of the house with briquettes that you took out of the barbecue? You thought they were already cold, but they weren't, and you burnt your fingers. You can't go through life being accident prone."

I, the young smart-aleck, was ready for this. I turned my pain into something snide and thus less painful.

"I know; you're going to tell me that I'm bound to go to jail and be fed dry bread and water. Which is worse, being accident prone or eating dry bread?"

I didn't know then what I know now, that I drew murals and made sculptures to manage my being accident prone.

"*Zie shtim.* Be quiet," said my mother.

Shortly thereafter, I was summoned by the principal, not to her usual office, but to a meeting room. A note had come to my teacher, Mrs. Fox, and I was sent without explanation, accompanied by a secretary. As far as I knew, the principal never talked to students. Formality reigned in school in those days. We did not call teachers by their first names; we didn't even *know* their first names. If by accident we learned a teacher's first name, we did not reveal what we knew. Mrs. Newman, the principal, did not have a knowable first name.

Entering the meeting room, I felt important. When I was in second grade, a painting I had done of a cow with huge udders was hung in the school's hallway outside her office. Perhaps she wanted to hang another painting of mine. Or was she worried about how I was doing with one crippled arm and one in a cast?

As I entered, I was surprised to see several adults sitting around a table, their chairs turned toward Mrs. Newman. Mrs. Newman told me to roll up the sleeve of my left arm. Then she pointed at it, speaking words of which I have no memory. She pointed again, explaining something important.

To this day, I do not understand what problem I illustrated in the grammar schools of Los Angeles. Was the meeting about the management of damaged children? Did I need management? Or did I illustrate the possibility that damaged children might manage themselves, even with a cast on their one good arm? Was the fact that I was accident prone too much of a legal risk? I would have to ask Uncle Hy, my father's brother, the lawyer, the second oldest. Was I a danger to others? Might I, on the other hand, illustrate how Los Angeles schools could turn a mess of a child into a success?

I was escorted back to my classroom, deflated, ice coursing through my veins. But I had a remedy for my disappointment: I annulled the meeting. I had never been run over, scarred, or suffered keloids. I'd never been so stupid as to climb into the rafters to play war games. I'd never reached my hand into burning coals. I had never hammered my thumb while turning tin cans and lids into sculpture.

As I lay on the Brain Injury unit, I tried annulling what had brought me there.

CHAPTER TEN

I Stood on My Own Two Feet

Once more unto the breach, dear friends, once more,
Or close the wall up with our English dead!
– William Shakespeare, *Henry V,* act 3, scene 1

I HAD TO WORK HARD ON MY FIRST DAY WITH THE REHAB'S PHYSICAL therapists, three of whom instructed me how to use a sliding board to slither into a wheelchair. One petite therapist braced the wheelchair while one steadied the slider and one kept me from dropping to the floor. Safely on board, I was wheeled down the hall to the gym.

All three supported me as I was maneuvered onto an exercise machine for pumping legs and arms from a seated position. My left hip remained stiff as I pumped away, but it wasn't painful, as long as I didn't stay in one position too long. I was stiff everywhere, having been bedbound for weeks.

Vicky signed me out for weekend therapy with the command, "Stretch the hell out of him."

One morning I was awakened according to the set routine, my breakfast clanging down on the bedside table. I wanted to eat heartily, but I couldn't, falling back into a sleepless stupor before forcing myself to eat and prepare for physical therapy. I had already been rehabbed enough to get myself ready for the gym by sleeping in gym shorts and a sleeveless exercise shirt. I was now making progress toward putting on my shoes and socks, now almost able to cross one leg over the opposite knee and rotate my foot into position to accept a shoe. I still had to ask for help from the nursing assistant. I promised myself to order more protein when I filled out forms for the next day's meals.

Vicky guided me to the gym and helped me struggle onto the stretching table. The painful stretching was supposed to help me uncoil. Relieved from stretching, I was helped onto the soft-seated, old-lady cycling machine, where I peddled with two feet and pumped the handles, holding on for life.

Exercising like this for two weeks won me the privilege of being given a walker, under the direction of my kind attending physician, Dr. Sean Song, who was indeed a song of hope. But he warned me not to take a step, "not yet." As I held on to my walker, I wagged my hips, rocking on my feet, fearful of lifting a single foot off the ground, but thrilled by being able to move even that much. "Not yet" was good enough for me.

Another physical therapist in the gym that day, Paul, whose name I had heard while he was working with other patients, came up to Dr. Song and said, "That man can walk." Paul radiated belief in my future, a belief that I'd been losing.

He said to me, "I'll come by your room after my last patient, about 4:30 or 4:45. I'll get you up to the parallel bars, and we'll see how far you can walk."

The idea that anybody could care that much about me at that time of day was beautiful, and the fact that he actually believed I would walk was thrilling. He was the first who understood my need to be reassured that I could walk.

As I waited patiently for Paul, Josie, one of my favorite nurses, came in with an early milkshake.

"Paul apologizes for not being able to come. He got called into a meeting, and after that, he had to go home. He said that because it's Friday and you won't want to wait to Monday, he is sending another therapist to get you up to the parallel bars this weekend. You will walk."

And that weekend, I did. The weekend therapist got me up to the parallel bars. I walked four steps forward—then five, shorter, careful steps backward, elated. My daughter Margaret wrote in the family blog, "A big day for Avi; he took four steps forward and five steps backward." I did not mind the ambiguous suggestion that my progress, however positive, might slip backward.

Once I could walk again, however clumsily with a walker, Vicky Stevens said, "When you were transferred here from Harborview, all the therapists here thought you were an inappropriate admission. You still had a feeding tube in, and you couldn't sit up. We were not permitted to get you to your feet, even if that were possible with full assistance, which it was not, because of your fractures. No weight-bearing was allowed. 'What the hell are we going to do with him?' we all asked. And here you are, our fastest in recovery."

Dr. Kurt Johnson, the expert on returning high-functioning professionals to work, told me that he and his colleagues feared I would never be able to return to my medical practice because I might not recover the physical agility to perform a neurologic exam, let alone manage the problem of my brain injury. When the Chairwoman of the Department of Rehabilitation Medicine, the kind and wise Dr. Kathleen Bell, eventually did recommend that I could return to work, she wrote, "He is the model of hard work." I had no other choice. Hard work on its own would do little without my brain's capacity to shape failures into semi-graceful walking.

By the time the able therapists finished with me, after extensive inpatient and then outpatient work, I ran a hundred yards, not at all fast, but I ran. At first, I thought that my chance of ever running again was not worth a hope. For weeks, while confined to my bed, pain kept me changing position every few minutes, vainly seeking a comfortable place. I did not manage to have a normal night's sleep during my two months in rehab.

Additional problems seemed likely to keep me from going back to my medical practice. My swallowing muscles had been injured when I was intubated in the field in Kenya. The breathing tube, slid between my vocal cords, had impaired my ability to keep food out of my lungs. I was thus confined to thickened fluids and was forbidden water and other thin fluids, for water is the hardest food to swallow safely. To be swallowed, liquid has to be balled up like solid food, rounded into a tidy "bolus," not a simple task. Before I could eat a regular diet, I had to prove on video that I could swallow safely. The first time I took the test, a dribble of fluid sloshed down toward my lungs. I didn't notice it since I did not cough, but there it was on the video, "silent aspiration," as pointed out by the polite Dr. Albert Merati, chief of Laryngology.

"We'll have to do it again. Every time you swallow, turn your head to the right and then the left; that will strengthen your pharyngeal muscles. Work on it. If it doesn't work, I can inject the muscles to strengthen them."

I did work on alternating my head position with every swallow without noticing any choking or coughing, nor any obvious improvement. But I did pass the repeat test, and so, was allowed whatever I wanted for meals. Because I had lost twenty-seven pounds, mainly from disuse atrophy of muscle, I ordered cheesecake for dessert, lunch, and dinner—not the right choice to put on muscle, but that's what I ordered. Kind Josie also ordered up from the kitchen my ice cream of choice, usually strawberry, my childhood favorite, and from the ice cream and her own ingredients, she hand-prepared milkshakes nightly, which were very helpful for walking. I knew I was pathetic, but I ordered milkshakes and cheesecake anyway.

When I clonked with my walker down the corridor to the gym, Vicky kept a sharp eye on me.

"I think we can try Lofstrand crutches soon," she offered optimistically.

"What are those?"

"Some people call them Canadian crutches."

"Oh, right, those. That's what I call them."

Relearning to walk and swallow allowed me to focus on my admitting diagnosis. Standing on one's own two feet involves more than the ability to walk. Walking is a metaphor. One says, "He knows where he is going" or "He is well on his way" or "He is off track" or "He is not up to speed" or "He was so lost I had to tell him to take a hike." I had been admitted to rehab not as a man with a gait disturbance, but as a brain-injured patient, a specialty at UW.

I was lucky to get there, for the orthopedists and the neurosurgeons at Harborview, having decided that I was not a surgical candidate, recommended that I be sent to a skilled nursing facility (an SNF, in medical jargon). My daughter Margaret insisted on rehab, recruiting to her plans Dr. Christian Shenouda, a young physiatrist, who, despite my ruinous deficits and the grave prognoses of others, saw in me hints that I could recover.

Because I had suffered head trauma, with a skull fracture and bleeding into my brain, I had to be tested and retested to show that I could cogitate. Having to prove that you are not permanently brain damaged is daunting and damaging in itself. I kept thinking that my challenge was close to that of those Russian intellectuals who, because they had uttered a single syllable that could be interpreted as criticism of *The Soviet Paradise,* were committed to pseudo psychiatric hospitals. Worse, I knew from my own professional experience that I was, in fact, brain injured and would prove myself so by conveying any hint that I thought otherwise. Brain-injured patients are notorious for thinking there is nothing wrong with them. I would need to be careful about not appearing overly confident, and this carefulness made me perseverative about my worries, to the point that I proved that I was indeed brain injured.

Andrea, having worked me through "silent aspiration," now turned to "speech," which was really "cognition." She warned me again and again to monitor my verbosity because my doctors would interpret this as ongoing proof of cognitive insufficiency. To get me to stay focused, she started waking me from naps to give me seven random words to remember. Most of the time, I could recall seven, but later on, I was required to remember twelve random words.

I never, then or in the past, had been interested in the random, but when I realized that I would never go back to work until I performed well in these irritating exercises, I committed myself to acquiring an interest in the random. And I could not lose my temper, no matter what. How often was I asked to work through a random problem? Probably five times a week for two months, and then as an outpatient. Among many other riddles, I solved the dilemma of an orchestra conductor arranging a schedule of concerts to please not only himself, but also the musicians, donors, subscribers, and corporate sponsors, with attention given to everyone's unusual preferences.

Andrea would say to me professionally, "I want to tell you a story. I will ask you to tell it back to me." A story would go something like this, as I recalled over a year later: "There was a storm near Albany, New York, with unusual rainfall. Rivers flooded. More than one hundred homes were destroyed, and six people died. A boy was swept away by the river, but a fireman was able to rescue him under a bridge, where the boy was trapped. The fireman injured his hand, but neither he nor the boy was otherwise hurt." Having been a professor of English literature, I could play this game fairly well.

But cognitive therapy turned more "serious." That is, I graduated to solving more complex word puzzles. I was put to work solving puzzles such as this one, now recalled imprecisely: "A woman is giving a party. She has eight guests, and she has prepared party favors for them all. Using the following twelve clues, determine which guests went home with which party favors." The clues included, among other fascinating facts, the announcement that Ann traded her candied apple for Steven's chocolate bar and that no two women took home the same gift, as well as other, sufficient information to answer the question. I supposed that my examiners thought this was cognitively no different from what I did on a daily basis, sorting through differential diagnoses of neurological syndromes. But there was this difference: The task before me, though clearly not mindless, did not engage my mind. Entertainment doesn't entertain me. Random puzzles and the thrill of solving them do not puzzle or thrill me.

As a matter of neurologic fact, the cognitive part of the brain has only a limited authority over the limbic system, that part of the brain that marks what is important to remember and what is to be disregarded, the very part of the brain that choses what we like and what we detest, what thrills us and what bores us, what we pursue and what we neglect. The old saying that there's no accounting for taste is not true. The accountant is in the limbic system, and my limbic system was not validating the importance of word puzzles about who took home which party favors.

The limbic system will not be easily instructed. Rather, it tells the cognitive system how to pursue pleasure, be it to score a symphony or score more heroin. The limbic system is a hedonist, a

Sybaritic governor of what Freud called the pleasure principle, that overpowering boss of what one likes and what one doesn't like. What the boss likes, the boss gets. What the boss doesn't like is censored, excommunicated, banished, expelled, forgotten.

Eventually, I was asked to read and discuss a medical article. After doing a passing job at this task, I was told this: "When you are in your arena, you do fine, but when you are in an unfamiliar arena, you can't put together a lot of new information fast enough. We can help you with this problem."

I knew that if I complained, I dug myself deeper into pathologic verbosity. I thought of Kafka's *The Trial.* The novel's protagonist, Josef K., could never extricate himself from presumed guilt, for he was like the Jewish Kafka, irrationally branded guilty, no matter what.

Of course, I was then in a state of despondency, and that was part of why I was so repetitive about my plight. But, after all, I was not Josef K., and I was, in fact, getting better. My therapists and nurses liked me. I would have to buck up and stifle my repetitive yakking, or so I repeatedly told myself.

And this brought to mind memories of my fears, fantasies, and foolery at the Mayo Clinic, where I underwent surgery to remove the large keloid from my right ear, the one that could hear.

CHAPTER ELEVEN

Mayo Clinic, Age Nine

I do beseech you
Let me o'erleap that custom, for I cannot
Put on the gown, stand naked, and entreat them,
For my wounds' sake, to give their suffrage.
– William Shakespeare, *Coriolanus,* act 2, scene 2

In December 1953, at the Mayo Clinic in Rochester, Minnesota, my mother was called in to Dr. Figi's office to discuss the keloid on my right ear. She handed me her newspaper and said, "Here, read this story while I talk to the doctor."

On the front page was the story of a bad accident. Three boys had fallen through thin ice while skating, and had died. Two firemen had also died while trying to rescue them. The firemen had slithered on their bellies over the ice, distributing their weight to avoid breaking through, but they'd fallen into the frozen water anyway. The continuation of this bad news appeared further on in the newspaper, where I also read an interview with the father of Anne Frank, who died on the very day I was born. Anne had been a skilled diarist, but her quiet, secret writing, her art, hadn't been able to save her.

I put down the paper and went to the window to watch snow falling on rooftops, a novel experience for a child from Los Angeles. Dr. Figi said a keloid was a kind of "overhealing," but to me, a keloid was a lash of shame. Twice in Los Angeles, doctors had tried to remove the orange-sized growth from my ear, but it grew back even bigger.

Dr. Figi was a tiny man whose hands shook. This worried me, but I liked that there was something wrong with him. His hands were delicate, but they trembled. My mother said that a nurse had assured her that they never shook during surgery.

I had persuaded my mother to agree that I wouldn't have to undergo surgery if I didn't want it, but I doubted I would be able to enforce this agreement. We had come a long way from Los Angeles on a new DC-7. Dr. Figi, who had taken a picture of the ear and its orange, wouldn't want to leave it as it was. There was supposed to be an "after" picture.

When I'd had the keloid removed two years before, the surgeon gave me a book he had written on surgery for noses. Puzzlingly, the book cover displayed pictures of dog snouts. Now the keloid was back, and we'd come all this way to remove it.

On the brain injury ward, I could see a good reason for my having been given a book with pictures of dog snouts, for I, in fact, was a dying dog.

As I stood by the window looking at the snow falling over Rochester, I discovered that my vision was getting worse. My mother had told me that I was nearsighted, and this made sense, as I could see near objects, like my own hand, but I couldn't see distant houses clearly as they spread out from the Mayo tower. I had also discovered how much my vision could be improved by making a pinhole lens. If I curled up my right index finger just so, I could let just a thin beam of light come through the tiny hole where the curled finger's creases met to make a bird's footprint, just like those in the snow on the very windowsill in front of me. When I held up this lens to my eye as a monocle, the blowing snow resolved into flakes.

I compared my vision through one eye alone to what I saw through the other eye alone. What I saw with one eye could not be superimposed on what I saw with the other eye. I could not make myself use both eyes at the same time. As I shifted from one eye to the other, the visual field moved ever so slightly along the horizon. It would take me twenty-five years to learn that this phenomenon had a name, "alternating strabismus," but I was able to describe it clearly at the Mayo Clinic. I found that if I lined up a vertical edge of a windowpane with the chimney across the way and then opened and shut each eye, I could make the chimney move from one pane to the next. I hoped that other kids saw the same shifts, that I wasn't abnormal.

My mother and Dr. Figi walked out of his office. Dr. Figi said I was scheduled for surgery to remove the keloid. I said no, but secretly,

I wanted to see the "after" picture. I was ashamed of the growth and wanted a new picture. Nevertheless, I pushed my pinhole-monocle into my eye and cried. Dr. Figi patted my head and left.

My mother said, "The nurses told me he is very good, very experienced. There's no substitute for experience. You'll see."

I told my mother that I could make eyeglasses out of my fingers.

"That's not possible. You don't have the *saychel* you were born with."

Saychel is the Yiddish word for the kind of understanding Jews were supposed to have but often didn't. My grandmother, my father's mother, often said, "In Yiddish, there is a word for everything." As a nine-year-old at the Mayo Clinic, looking out on snowflakes and chimney bricks, I thought my *saychel* was pretty good. I could not have known at the time that my mother's use of the word *saychel* referred to the modern neurological idea of a well-tuned executive function humming away in the antero-mesial frontal lobes of the human brain.

I showed my mother how to make a lens with her curled index finger.

"Try it," I said. "You're nearsighted too."

She did and was surprised.

"Oh, my God, you're right!" she said.

Encouraged, I asked, "What do you call the piece of wood that separates the windowpanes?" Focusing on the name of these slender slats was better than fretting about surgery on my slender ear with its big keloid.

"Why do you ask?"

"I just want to know. Look there, at the window slats. What is the word?"

I was afraid to tell her that I saw the chimney in different panes when I looked through alternating eyes. There was a word for that, I was sure, and a surgeon too, equipped with ether anesthetic, so I never told my mother about my alternating strabismus.

We stayed at the Zumbro Hotel, an old-fashioned place with writing desks in the lobby. Intricately carved wooden dividers made each desk private, with inkwells, blotting paper, stationery, and a roll of stickers that read "Via Airmail." I wrote my father, but the letter came back for insufficient postage. I'd thought a Via Airmail sticker *was* postage.

A heavy unabridged dictionary sat on an oak stand near the desks. Under the word *window,* I found detailed illustrations of windows and the word *came,* which is a lead bar that separates panes in stained-glass windows. I found *mullion* and *transom,* horizontal and vertical separators of panes, different words for the same thing in different directions. I also looked up *abridged,* learning that I was to have my keloid abridged.

In Rochester, Minnesota, the weather was often too cold to walk on the surface streets, so my mother and I used the network of tunnels that connected the Mayo Clinic to several hotels and other medical buildings. My mother could not navigate without me. She got lost, couldn't remember the turns, and thought the landmarks all looked alike. I had to tell her which way to go.

I felt proud when she asked, "Are you sure?"

"Don't you remember? You looked in this window and liked that coat."

"Yes, I did like that coat, but it's not the same coming from this direction."

I worried about her *saychel.*

My mother and I met a Jewish family from Omaha who had brought their daughter to the clinic for treatment. I thought her pretty, dark, and serious. She taught me to write in code by using a dot placed in various places in the tic-tac-toe grid to indicate every letter. She showed me how to compress the code, using the unique shape of every square in the grid to signal which square we were using, without having to draw the whole grid. The square in the middle, for example, was reduced to just that, a four-sided figure, while the upper right square looked like a big L, the upper middle square like a big U. That U, with a dot in the middle of its base, represented the letter E, for my last name. At first, this was fun. Then it became tedious. I thought of this code when my cognitive therapists asked me to solve word puzzles, childish and reeking of bad memories.

In code, I asked the lovely Miss Omaha what was wrong with her, but she never told me. I assumed she was dying. But she went home, still sure of herself. I wrote to her to see if she'd died, and she wrote back in code, saying she was well. I didn't believe her.

In the evenings, my mother and I went out for tuna sandwiches because it was too expensive to eat in the hotel. My breath steamed in the streets, and my ears burned with cold. I was a man, because I felt snow fall on me, as had my father in the Battle of the Bulge.

"What makes my breath steam?" I asked my mother.

"When I was a girl in Winnipeg, we would spit in the winter, and it would freeze before it hit the ground. It would go 'ping' on the sidewalk."

"But what makes my breath steam?"

"The same thing; it freezes. The water vapor in your breath freezes into tiny droplets, too tiny to fall and go 'ping.' It just condenses. In Winnipeg, snow stayed on the ground so long that I lost a ring in November and didn't find it until the snow melted in May. I was so happy when I found that ring."

Suddenly, I was in a hospital again, this one, a Catholic hospital, much older than any hospital in Los Angeles. It had fancier doorways and moldings and had been built for a harsher climate, with hissing radiators. I let the nuns know that I disapproved of the crucifix over my bed without saying anything to them. I made them run me down at bedtime. I wouldn't cooperate with bathing. I wouldn't smile back at them when they smiled at me.

I liked my tall, skinny roommate, Roger, with his red crew cut because he was unhappy, gloomy. He suffered from chronic diarrhea, an embarrassment that I did not count as a disease, not knowing any better. He often went into the bathroom, expelled a lot of gas, flushed the toilet, and came out, pale and skinnier than ever. Sweat beaded on his forehead and on his red hair.

"Why do you eat all that stew and not get sick?" he asked me. "I shit! You don't."

Roger was being mean, but he didn't look mean—just pale, skinny, sweaty, and trembling. He looked like he had enough to worry about without tormenting me. What would I have thought if I'd had diarrhea instead of keloids?

After Roger went home, still with diarrhea, I stopped moving my bowels to prove I didn't have diarrhea. I wanted control. I didn't want my temperature checked every shift. I stood in a doorway under a crucifix, squeezed my butt cheeks together, waiting for my rumblings to stop.

The departure of gloomy Roger made room for Tommy, a boy whose nose was burnt off, along with much of his face. He had already undergone many skin grafts, and he was going to get a doctor-built nose too. For now, he had no nose, just two holes instead of nostrils. My mother told me that she had read about him in the newspaper. His house had caught fire. According to her, the deeper parts of his nostrils still worked.

Tommy was eight, a year younger than I. I was nice to him, but I preferred escaping into *The Adventures of Tom Sawyer,* where I found a healthy Tom. Tommy had no eyebrows, eyelids, or hair. I learned a way to look at him and keep a normal expression so he wouldn't know that his appearance scared me.

One of the other children on my floor was making belts from kits. Precut tabs of leather fit ingeniously together to make a handsome product. I started making belts too, taking orders from other patients' parents. Tommy tried to make belts as well, but his fingers were skin-grafted sticks, too clumsy. I had often been asked if I had been burned, since my keloids looked like burn scars. As I glanced furtively at Tommy, I was glad that I had not been burned, especially given my pyromania.

The nuns tried to get me to go to sleep, but I stayed up late reading and making belts, using the light that came in from the hallway. I thought that if I'd had Tom Sawyer's craftiness, I wouldn't be in this fix.

The morning of my surgery came quickly enough. Again, I would undergo the terrifying smother of ether. But this time, I at least knew that no harm was intended. Dr. Figi promised me that the anesthesiologists would give me a pill to make me go to sleep while

I was still in my room, so that when I got to the operating room, I wouldn't even notice the ether. And, indeed, an anesthesiologist came to my room with a pill. But I didn't fall asleep in my room. I continued reading *The Adventures of Tom Sawyer.*

When the anesthesiologist came back to see if I was asleep, he said, surprised, "That must be some book! If you can stay awake through all the stuff I'm giving you, either the book is terrific, or your concentration is."

I was hardly asleep at all when the stinking towel of ether dropped over me. The foul stench of this supposed kindness snuffed out the desperation of Tom Sawyer trapped in the dark cave. The sun-bright lamps over the operating table went dim, permitting a painless clipping of the keloid.

I remained in the hospital after surgery. Dr. Figi wanted me there for dressing changes. As the nuns pulled the dressing off, they said it would hurt only for a second; then they added, "It's coming along fine."

One morning I woke to find a sign hanging from my headboard: "Prepare for Surgery." I was terrified. Ice coursed through my veins. Already, the vicious metal light was boring through my eyelids and lighting up a passage for the ether. I couldn't take any more ether. Something had gone dreadfully wrong with my ear. The dressing felt the same as before. I wondered, *Why does Dr. Figi think I need more surgery without even waiting to see how the last surgery turned out?*

A nun came into my room.

"Why do I have to have more surgery?" I asked her.

"Who says you're having surgery?"

"That sign."

"Oh, that just means it's you who is going to get the dressing change."

"You never put up one of those signs before."

"We have some substitutes in the hospital for Christmas, very nice young nuns. So many of our regulars are away for the holidays, just as you are away from school for Christmas vacation. We decided to put up signs to avoid any mistakes. We don't want a sweet girl changing the wrong boy's dressing by accident, do we?"

She ripped the sign off, then the dressing.

"Now doesn't that look nice?" she asked, marching me over to the mirror above the sink in the corner.

And there was my ear, almost normal looking, with a little scab at the top.

"Dr. Figi told me that we can now leave the dressing off."

During the day I picked at the scab until it fell off. I was afraid it would bleed, but it didn't. I watched for my mother from my window, which was directly over the hospital entrance. The hospital was shaped like the letter U, with the entrance at the bottom of the letter, far from the street. By using my finger lens, I could watch my mother cut through the U.

I was feeling happy until my mother brought in a shoebox of get-well cards from my classmates in Miss Schaff's fourth grade. I liked Miss Schaff, especially since she hung my paintings in class. But now I felt betrayed. I'd assumed that my classmates were not paying attention to my prolonged absence, not thinking of me at all. I had left for Christmas vacation, and then a little more, no big deal, even if nobody else was flying to Minnesota. What could they know about Roger's diarrhea and Tommy's nostrils? Nothing.

But they did know I was in Rochester having surgery! Of course they would know; they'd seen my orange. And now I had to read their cards. Those from the boys were not so bad. But the girls wrote long letters on pink stationery. They told me about the stuff I had missed. This was grim. I wanted them to think of me as normal, but they thought I was damaged.

On my last day in the hospital, Dr. Figi took a picture. When he held the camera up, his hands stopped shaking. Perhaps he suffered from tremor-dominant Parkinson's disease. The picture lifted a measure of shame from me. My right ear now appeared almost normal, and it worked well. The left ear remained deaf, but it looked perfect.

CHAPTER TWELVE

My Own Physician

MACBETH: Canst thou not minister to a mind diseas'd;
Pluck from the memory a rooted sorrow;
Raze out the written troubles of the brain;
And, with some sweet oblivious antidote,
Cleanse the stuff'd bosom of the perilous stuff
Which weighs upon the heart?
DOCTOR: Therein the patient
Must minister to himself.

– William Shakespeare, *Macbeth,* act 5, scene 3

In rehab, I occasionally tried to doctor myself. Macbeth, I recalled, asks Lady Macbeth's doctor if he cannot cure his wife's diseased mind, but the good doctor reminds the usurping king that there are times when the "patient must minister to himself." The physician can only hint that Macbeth, too, has a "mind diseased," for he uses the male pronoun "himself." The Thane of Cawdor shares his wife's disease; after all, she carries his name.

In rehab, I was forced to wear a sterile gown when I left my room, and my visitors also had to don this stifling protection to avoid being contaminated by me. The gown and gloves made me perspire insufferably when I was brought to the gym to exercise. I was informed that I had told a nurse that I was infected by methicillin-resistant Staphylococcus aureus (MRSA), the dreaded bacterium that, because it is resistant to so many antibiotics, can be fatal. I was sure that I myself had never cultured positive for MRSA, that even in a brain-injured state I could not have told anybody about my MRSA status. But, then again, I was so unsure of myself that I doubted my brain-injured memory.

Then I was told that the hospital had indeed cultured MRSA from my nostrils, where the nasty bacteria often lurk. Nobody could show me the report of my supposedly positive culture. I had enough sense to convince the harmonious Dr. Song to re-culture my nose and any other areas to prove that I did not harbor MRSA. I told him that I could not exercise while swaddled like a baby, cocooned, mummified, sealed from the touch of others.

My nose was re-swabbed and my urine was collected. With unsterile technique, I followed instructions to pee into a urinal open to contamination, the contents collected erratically.

Just as I thought I would never learn the results of my urine culture, Dr. Song caught me motoring myself along in my wheelchair, gowned so that I would not contaminate others. I was pleased to demonstrate a little speed.

He said, "Hey, where's the fire? And by the way, the only positive finding from your culture was some gram-negative rods in your urine that they can't identify."

Dr. Song didn't seem to be coming to the obvious conclusion, so I interrupted him, my affection for him failing to prevent me from being snide.

"Whatever these bacteria are, they are not MRSA. Staphylococcus aureus look like blue balls under the microscope, and what has been found look like red rods. Red rods can't be blue balls. And the red rods are probably due to contamination because the specimens were collected in a slovenly way."

"True. But, we must wait for the infectious-disease people to clear you."

"Please tell them I can't exercise in a gown and sterile gloves."

"I will tell them what you said."

A few days later, I was wearing gym shorts and a tank top, never so happy to expose my long-damaged left arm in the overheated gym. I asked my visiting brother-in-law, Marc, to bring me shorts and tank tops, and in that sartorial state, I lived and slept until I was discharged, no longer a mummy.

That problem solved, I turned to my being injected with Lovenox, a blood thinner, an indignity that occurred nightly at bedtime. A nurse took my blood pressure, and, without further ceremony, plunged a needle into the subcutaneous tissue of my abdomen. Since

I had ordered this treatment only for bedridden stroke victims in order to prevent clots from developing in their sluggish legs, I was aware that there is no reason to continue the injections after the patient is up and walking. I had gotten so used to this bedtime indignity that I forgot to complain. Finally, I told Dr. Song that I thought discontinuing the Lovenox was overdue.

He said, "Oh, I'm so sorry. I thought we'd already stopped it." The injections promptly ended.

Once I was allowed to drink clear liquids, I started ordering coffee with breakfast, joking with Dr. Song that I'd prescribed myself a new medicine, caffeine, and I thought that he should know that this was giving me more energy for my early morning bouts in the gym with Vicky. And every few days, I lowered my morphine further, waking myself from stupor.

I was now clear enough to recall that the only medicine I took regularly before my bike crash was allopurinol for mild gout. And since my past medical history was never taken in its entirety, I thought I should be my own doctor and alert Dr. Song. The next day, I got my allopurinol.

But this did nothing for my untethered pain emanating from my fractured left pelvis. I wanted ibuprofen, the over-the-counter anti-inflammatory that the orthopedists at my hospital used for patients who had suffered hip fractures, to avoid addicting them to opiates. I'd used the medication myself after arduous bike rides. The nurses kept telling me that they could not give ibuprofen to patients with fractures "because it interferes with bone healing."

This seemed ludicrous to me. Fortunately, an intelligent medical student was assigned to my case. I asked her to research the subject by using her computer access to the UW library. As I suspected, the evidence that anti-inflammatories inhibit the healing of fractured bones came from only a few, non-conclusive studies on animals, not humans. Some rabbits apparently heal fractures less well when given drugs like ibuprofen (but at doses much higher on a per-kilogram of weight than would ever be given to humans). The clever medical student then called the Department of Orthopedics and learned that their doctors routinely use ibuprofen six weeks after a fracture. I soon got four hundred milligrams thrice daily, at precisely specified times, as if getting the med thirty minutes too early might startle my pelvis. I thus made more progress.

It might have helped if I had been seen by an orthopedist once I was transferred from the excellent orthopedic care at Harborview Hospital (of which I still have no memory) to the University of Washington Hospital. I realized that patients, even *my* patients, can benefit from more attention to their understanding and expectations. All you have to do is ask them.

I asked if I could go to the gym without my physical therapist.

"For safety reasons, this is not permitted."

"Even if other therapists are there?"

"No."

CHAPTER

THIRTEEN

More Self-Doctoring, Age Eleven

The office of medicine is but to tune the curious harp of man's body and to reduce it to harmony.

– Sir Francis Bacon, *The Advancement of Learning*, 1605

I WOVE BEING MY OWN PHYSICIAN IN REHAB TOGETHER WITH OLDER memories of doctoring myself. My milk truck accident had already rendered my crushed left elbow unable to turn my palm upward, but by the age of eleven, I couldn't fully extend my elbow. The ropes of keloid had failed to grow with me. I thought I could cut parts of the keloids off painlessly because I had lost sensation in the area. I would be my own surgeon, and I wouldn't even need ether.

On the coffee table in our living room, my mother kept a set of silver nutcrackers that she'd received as a wedding gift. The set, which we never used, included a tong-like cracker and two picks. My plan was to pick off as much keloid as I could. I set to work immediately, not anticipating much bleeding from the tough, ropy tissue. But there was bleeding. I realized then that the keloids' purple color must be related to the fact that they possessed a blood supply. Soon I had to stop. I bandaged what I had done. When my mother asked me why I needed a bandage, I told her that I had scratched my elbow while climbing over the chain-link fence at Castle Heights Elementary to shoot baskets alone in the late afternoon.

My surgical site got infected with pus. I thought I might die, the way my friend Susan's sister died from mastoiditis, because bugs got into her brain. That was during the war, before antibiotics. I had to tell my mother about the pus so I could get antibiotics, but I didn't tell her I'd operated on myself.

She took me to a real surgeon, whose breath smelled of alcohol. I knew it was alcohol because of James, who helped my father haul poultry from the desert around Palmdale. He came to our house on Commonwealth Avenue to light firecrackers on the Fourth of July. James knew just how to arrange a firecracker under a tin can balanced on a washboard across the clothesline. The tin can would explode into the sky.

I asked my mother what made James's breath smell.

My mother said, "James drinks. On the Fourth of July, he drinks more."

The surgeon said he would remove some of the keloid and swing a flap of skin around to free more movement for the elbow. He said that he wouldn't remove all of the keloid because that would require too much skin grafting, and he couldn't fix my elbow because there wasn't a joint to fix.

"We can schedule the surgery in two weeks, after you graduate Castle Heights. You can start junior high school with a practically new arm, but it will always be shorter than your other one."

My mother saw that I hadn't yet faced the hard truth that my left arm was never going to catch up to the right. She focused on reassuring me about the necessity of the upcoming surgery.

"You can't walk around like that," she said. "Nobody is going to let you swim in their swimming pool with that running sore."

For graduation from Castle Heights, my mother gave me a V-necked wool sweater; it was wine colored, not purple, like the sweater I wore after my milk truck accident. I thought it looked handsome. I wore it to the Smith Brothers Restaurant with my parents. My siblings weren't invited to join us.

My mother told the waiter she didn't want a cocktail, but my father ordered something complicated, containing "gin." I ordered the filet of sole, which came with tartar sauce. The Tartars, a Turkish ethnic group I'd learned about, lived in Asia far from the ocean, so I wondered why they named the sauce after them.

"Why do they call it tartar sauce?" I asked my parents.

My father sneered, "Why 'tartar sauce'? Why, why. All you ever ask is why. Sometimes there is no why."

"Butchie," said my mother, "sometimes there is."

When he was in high school, my father was sweet and cheerful, a prankster with curly hair. His friend Frankie nicknamed him Butchie, because he was the opposite of a butch. He was definitely not a tough guy. His real name was David, like the King of Israel.

"The Tartars are ferocious," I said.

The alcoholic surgeon did a good job. My crippled arm looked better—not beautiful, but better.

During my training to become a physician, I could do everything well with my arms as they were. I actually became expert in putting in intravenous lines and doing lumbar punctures. But I knew I couldn't become a surgeon, as I was unable to manage delicate suturing, with one hand limited in its mobility and my inability to use both eyes at the same time, thus with limited depth perception. I needed to lean far over the patient in order to suture proficiently, so the surgeons, fearful that I was contaminating the surgical field, rightfully stopped asking me to help.

As a patient in rehab, I knew that to recover, I had to marshal what skills I had, just as I'd tried to reassure my patients that they could bring together their own creative efforts to enhance their chances of recovery.

CHAPTER FOURTEEN

A Shakespearean Fantasizes

Young men will do't, if they come to 't
By Cock, they are to blame.

– William Shakespeare, *Hamlet,* act 4, scene 5

In rehab, Shakespeare was my escape. As I composed thoughts about his plays, I realized that I had new ideas. This in turn gave me confidence that by weaving my thoughts, I could help rehabilitate my mind. Creating ideas enriches one's capacity to create more ideas.

Throughout his career, Shakespeare wrote iteratively about the loss of stature, power, esteem, of the capacity to understand, from the bewildered twins in *The Comedy of Errors,* who, of course, cannot know that as characters in a play. They represent a single but divided, unhinged mind. This is also true of the easily deluded Othello, the besotted Antony, and the self-infantilized King Lear, all suffering the consequences of an unruly executive function, just the subject that preoccupied me. Shakespeare wrote about uncontrollable ambitions and lust, about hungers of all kinds in all combinations. He wrote of deadly sex and violence in *Romeo and Juliet,* in *Troilus and Cressida,* and in *Antony and Cleopatra.* He wrote of love and sadomasochism in *Titus Andronicus, Othello, King Lear,* and *Cymbeline.* And does not Richard III believe that with his superior cleverness he can successfully disguise his maniacal lust to rule by coating it with sweet talk? Early in the play named after him, Richard III persuades the lovely Lady Anne, who is, herself, in the line of inheritance to the throne and whose husband he has killed, to accept him as her new husband. Little does he know that he is outsmarting himself, making himself hateful as he executes the first steps toward his own demise.

These memories of Richard's cunning love and Romeo's desperate love, of Queen Mab and of the magic in the web of Othello's mother's fatal hankie, provoked in me vivid fantasies as I lay undone. I share these embarrassing fantasies now to illustrate what goes on in the mind of a long-confined man.

Doctors do not often ask patients about their thoughts, and almost never about their fantasies. But thoughts and fantasies are active anyway. Used creatively, they can be therapeutic. Fantasies demonstrate a capacity to fashion a coherent whole, with all aspects fitting together. Specific fantasies about manliness can support efforts to return to manliness, to keep hope alive and realistic.

Even if a fantasy is unrealistic, the brain might make use of it as it mobilizes its plastic power to reorganize itself. The risk, of course, is that undisciplined fantasies become a mere escape—or worse, delusional and self-destructive, as in the case of Julius Caesar.

This ambitious general who daringly crossed the Rubicon then suffers from self-imposed blindness as he marches obliviously to his death. He heeds neither the warnings of his friends, nor of the soothsayer, nor of his wife, who foresees all. He cannot recall his own frailties, his having to be rescued from drowning ("Help me, Cassius, or I sink!"), his seizure disorder, his having to station his infertile wife before the parading Antony so that she might conceive, and his deafness in his left ear (like me, Caesar says, "Come on my right side, for this ear is deaf"). He thinks he is "constant as the Northern Star," that he and Danger "are two lions littered in one day, and I the elder and more terrible," but he proves himself to be a slaughtered whelp.

In a dreamlike state, I recalled the time when I started teaching at Queens College, part of the City University of New York (CUNY—an acronym that now tickled my mind salaciously). There, I met the wife of a part-time adjunct instructor of English composition. Dawn was tall and lissome. I was living in Greenwich Village, and Dawn came into the Village from New Jersey regularly for a dance class. We arranged nonchalantly to have lunch one day when she was in town and I was not teaching, and then we had lunch again. Nothing else occurred.

I recalled the sexual chemistry between us thirty-five years earlier, and I regretted my restraint, activated by collegiality. On that occasion, I resolved to be a gentleman. But in my current circumstances, I wildly remade history. I molded a rich panoply of detail into something that resembled pulp fiction, drawing on my literary bent. Though my capacity to weave this fantasy encouraged me to make further efforts toward recovery, this therapy is not for most patients.

In an upscale restaurant in New York's SoHo neighborhood, I said to Dawn rather stiffly, "Forgive me for bringing up a difficult subject. I find you immensely attractive, and I often fail to attend to what you are saying, because my mind wanders into fantasies of making love to you. If I sometimes seem distracted, it is because I am. I am truly sorry."

Since fabricated stories move rapidly, Dawn immediately replied, "Don't be sorry. I feel that way too."

"Can we be lovers without causing a disaster for your husband and your son?" I asked.

"I think so," she said.

We went back to my apartment on Sheridan Square. All was easy, lovely, not a difficult accomplishment if one is running the fantasy.

Lying in my arms, Dawn whispered, "I'm going to Atlantic City the weekend after next. A friend of mine, Elaine, who likes to gamble, likes me to keep her company. She pays for two rooms—one for me, one for her. Sometimes she meets a guy. She likes to be in her own room anyway. Can you join me there? My daughter will be with her grandparents in Florida, and I'll have a bit of time for myself."

My fantasizing mind seems to have woven a magic carpet from wishful patches, with details materializing willy-nilly. Yet the weave was coherent in its own way, a rehearsal of the rehabilitated capacity I needed, a preview of the rebirth of a literary and medical man, of an astute reader of themes and symptoms.

I now see how vacuous was the drama I composed, but I enjoyed it anyway, like a drunkard. None of my characters showed any real emotion. Nobody was truly aroused. The sex wasn't sexy. All was matter-of-fact, without urgency or joy. And I, the oblivious conductor, could hear no music coming from my orchestra, for I was making none. Because I was a dying dog, I was less than a dog, an example of the limbic system untethered.

My father, who ran a kosher poultry plant on Santa Monica Boulevard in Hollywood, had set up a candling station for our retail customers, in a closet behind the display case at the front of the plant. Candling eggs allows one to discard eggs with blood spots in them. Over the candling light hung a calendar with airbrushed photographs of naked movie stars, one for each month, smiling sweetly with pseudo sexuality, Hollywood style. I gawked at Lana Turner's erect nipples.

As a pubescent teen, I often pictured those breasts. During that time, Lana Turner's daughter took a knife and murdered her mother's lover, Johnny Stompanato Jr. My mother told me that he, a thug, had been appropriately stabbed with a ten-inch knife.

She added, "He was an Italian, a mafioso—no Romeo."

CHAPTER FIFTEEN

A Turkish Dog

O damned Iago. O inhuman dog!

– William Shakespeare, *Othello,* act 5, scene 1

MY UNLEASHED SEXUAL FANTASIES MADE ME FEEL NEEDY AND PATHETIC, a dying dog that was gnawing on an imaginary bone, kenneled, darting back and forth between imaginary sex and all-too-possible death. For all my improvement in rehab, I was far from my former self. I could not see how my "rapid progress" was going to recreate a physician who worked long hours.

I was in no mood for Shakespeare, but there he was. Uninvited,

Othello barged into my brooding, likening himself to a Turkish dog. To his former admirers, now his keepers, the despondent murderer of his innocent wife dictates his last will as he is about to kill himself: "Set you down this / And say besides, that in Aleppo once, / Where a malignant and a turban'd Turk / Beat a Venetian and traduced the state, / I took by the throat the circumcised dog, / And smote him, thus."

And there I was, a dying circumcised dog like Othello's Turk, bound to death. He was dead from being manipulated, I from an accident. Oh, accidents! Did not Othello himself once turn the tale of his many accidents into the very power that won the love of Desdemona? Desdemona hinted that she wanted to hear his tale. And tell, he did:

> I spoke of most disastrous chances:
> Of moving accidents by flood and field,
> Of hair-breadth 'scapes i' th' imminent deadly breach,
> Of being taken by the insolent foe
> And sold to slavery, of my redemption thence. . . .
> These things to hear
> Would Desdemona seriously incline.

Now, why did chance and accident once favor him but now unmake him? Just by chance did Iago obtain the handkerchief that Othello gave Desdemona, a gift that Othello had been given by his mother, who in turn had received it from an Egyptian charmer who "could almost read the thoughts of people." The charmer, who promised that the handkerchief could subdue the fury of a libidinous husband, had gotten it from an aged sibyl who sewed it in "prophetic fury." "There's magic in the web of it," Othello warns Desdemona. Losing it is "such perdition / As nothing else could match."

With this magic handkerchief in hand, Othello binds Desdemona to him, and Iago undoes Othello with this very magic. What is this "magic in the web"? I couldn't remember what I'd made of it in the past. I couldn't remember because my mind was dying. Then I had an insight, a lifesaving insight! However dead I was, I couldn't be that dead, because I had an insight, even if it were misconceived. Did not Descartes already prove that I could not be a dead dog? "Cogito, ergo sum," he famously said. I think, therefore I am not dead.

My insight was this. A well-woven mind has the magic to weave life's mess into a web with power to subdue the fury that prevails in the world and in the mind. The magic in the web is the power of a well-orchestrated mind. The harmonized mind possesses understanding, which allows for well-executed behavior, makes military battles successful, parries slander, and facilitates the poetic wooing of the lovely Desdemona. The loss of executive function is the perdition that nothing else can match, the hell of not being able to penetrate the machinations of Iago, of not being able to catch the machinations of one's own mind. Othello says that his mother's handkerchief could "subdue my father entirely to her love," but no handkerchief can do this, and no loss of a handkerchief can, by itself, do any harm. But the loss of a healthy web of mind can. This, I believed, was Shakespeare's point, an offering even to me. If I could use my synthesizing mind to understand Othello, I could use the same power to master myself.

Executive function is just that ability of the mind to consider the panoply of past and present experience and then harmonize the whole, leading to well-conceived action. That is what we understand in the field of neurology. That is what the brain can do in the best of circumstances. And that is what Shakespeare understood, with no help from the psychology of his age. No psychologist in the sixteenth and seventeenth centuries was interested in how the brain fashioned well-woven action out of a tangled web of past experiences and present dangers.

The play's tragedy is the failure of Othello, the warrior of superstitious Moorish ancestry to integrate fully into the higher civilization of Venice, his employer. His task was to harmonize his uncouth background with civilized skill. This synthesis is actually captured in the play's title, *Othello, the Moor of Venice;* the title character is both Moorish and Venetian. The handkerchief itself is a weave of Moorish superstition and Venetian civilization. The two-hundred-year-old sibyl sewed with a "prophetic fury" derived from both a gory pagan religion and the science of Galileo, who happened to be born in the same year as Shakespeare, 1564. Of course, Othello, only half civilized, with minimal knowledge of astronomy, misunderstands Galileo, still thinking that the sun "compasses" the earth, and he blindly accepts the preposterous notion that a potent dye can be skillfully obtained from "maidens' hearts." Othello's weave of this misbegotten mini-tapestry reveals a mind prepared to be further misled by Iago's clever turning of the handkerchief against the Moor's mental web, which is already perverse.

'Tis true, there's magic in the web of it.
A sibyl, that had numbered in the world
The sun to course two hundred compasses,
In her prophetic fury sewed the work.
The worms were hallowed that did breed the silk,
And it was dyed in mummy which the skillful
Conserved of maidens' hearts

However superstitious Elizabethans might have been, Shakespeare could not have expected his audience to take as fact that there was mummified magic in the web of Othello's mother's Egyptian handkerchief. He might hope that his audience would understand that what undid Othello was the unweaving of the magic in the web of his mind, the loss of the power that once allowed him to outmaneuver "the Cannibals that each other eat."

Before it unraveled, his intact mind allowed him to weave accident into wooing, and wooing into the bonds of life and love. The loss of *this* magic is what turns a man into a violent Turkish dog, a cannibal who has consumed himself, much to the shock of his fellow Venetians. Near the end, Lodovico asks, "Is this the noble Moor whom our full senate / Call all in all sufficient?" Rabid and self-destructive, Othello is a failed man, without the ability to use his art to master his bedeviled rage. He is indeed correct when he moans, "I am not valiant neither, / But every puny whipster gets my sword." My thought that Othello's valiant capacity devolved into self-destruction enlivened my hope for the converse. I would revitalize myself with the art of a Victor, with superior executive function.

And did not Henri Rousseau show with his scandalous painting *Beauty and the Beast* that a creative mind can rise above the level of a libidinous dog? By portraying an assaulted woman improbably holding up a mirror as she is mounted by a dog, Rousseau alludes to Hamlet's advice to the actors who have come to court to perform the play within the play. The end of playing, says Hamlet, "was and is, to hold, as 'twere, the mirror up to nature." As the artfully painted Beauty holds up a mirror to the natural setting of her being taken by the Beast, she suggests that the creative mind can transcend perverse violation and thereby master outrageous fortune.

The memory of Rousseau's well-painted canvas reminded me that I could undertake the daunting challenge to elevate my own troubled mind.

By good fortune, at the moment I was fretting about the dogs within me, Dr. Kurt Johnson happened to drop by my room briefly, accompanied by his associate of the same name, spelled slightly differently, Dr. Curt Johnson. Dr. Curt, like his doppelganger, Dr. Kurt, expressed a belief that I was going to recover. He set up a computer and asked me to type.

"He types better than I do," said Curt to Kurt, making me think that I might just become myself again.

This capacity to telegraph to a patient a believable confidence in the possibility of recovery is not teachable. The young physician either has it or not, and as he matures, he will not acquire it if he lacked it at the beginning. In a magical way, Kurt and Curt represented to me that I, too, had a double self. There was more to me than met the eye. I was potentially a second, better version of myself, an Othello with his mind in possession of its handkerchief.

Of course, these doppelgangers' gift of projecting confidence cannot overcome mortality. There are hopeless cases. There are bad brain tumors and brains so shot up that no recovery can be expected. Nevertheless, the gifted physician is able to convey a comfort to his patient that everything that can be done will be done, that all may yet be rewoven.

How much of my recovery was due to my own artful weaving? How much was due to the standard program I was put through in rehab? How much was merely due to the tincture of time?

Might other patients with brain injury use their own creativity to facilitate recovery? What if the patient is not a neurologist and not a professor of literature? I didn't do an unbiased experiment of going through rehabilitation first without using my impulse to make a woven tapestry of the tangled threads of my plight, and then go through rehab again with no effort to compose. But I am quite sure that an effort to harmonize one's memories, fantasies, hopes, and terrors would help any patient with a similar injury. Most people have creative capacities, even if they're little used.

CHAPTER SIXTEEN

Building My Muscles, Age Thirteen

All audible musical sound is given us for the sake of harmony . . . which, as anyone who makes intelligent use of the arts knows, is not to be used, as is commonly thought, to give irrational pleasure, but as a heaven-sent ally in reducing to order and harmony any disharmony within us.

– Plato, *Timaeus*

In Los Angeles, at Louis Pasteur Junior High, I started building my muscles. I wanted to climb the twenty-foot pole in gym class. If I could climb that pole, I could work my way out of the lowest-level group, where the boys were either lazy or fat or disabled.

Every night I lifted my father's Underwood typewriter in its case one hundred times with each arm. On the linoleum floor of my bedroom, with its tangelo and turquoise flecks, I did twenty push-ups, then twenty-five, then thirty, then thirty-five. It was hard to do this with my left arm, but I worked at it and got stronger. In rehab, it helped me to draw on this memory.

Every week I got higher up the tall, slender pole. Eventually, I touched the top bar. Then I started aiming to climb the pole fast enough to earn the full twenty points on the test. I did these climbs with my palms facing away from the pole, since I couldn't rotate my left hand.

Overhand chin-ups are harder than underhand, but Mr. Powers counted them reluctantly. They didn't fit the protocol.

With my fast time climbing the pole, my twenty chin-ups, and my twenty push-ups, I scored enough points to make the highest level in gym class. That certainly pulled me up. Later in rehab, this memory again pulled me up, weaving itself into the rest of my story.

I was becoming a man. My crowd at Louis Pasteur started throwing regular parties, to which I was surprisingly invited. I knew how to dance. I began finding myself handsome. I looked into the mirror and saw a pleasant face. I held my fists in the air to better see how the right arm dwarfed the left, or the other way round, according to the uncanny reversal of the mirror.

Now that summer was coming, there would also be beach parties, and I was going to have to reveal my left arm. I had been keeping it covered ever since I started junior high, but I now thought that I should never have been secretive. I should have let anybody who didn't like what they saw go to hell. I now felt brave enough to refrain from wearing long sleeves on hot days.

That summer, I was reading *Romeo and Juliet* on my own, after liking *A Midsummer Night's Dream*, which was assigned to me the previous semester. I didn't understand much of *A Midsummer Night's Dream*, but I could tell it was grand, an aquarium full of new species, a galaxy of sparkling stars I never imagined, where strife and cruelty ended in laughter because of some mysterious order magically asserting itself in an otherwise topsy-turvy world.

Many decades later, in rehab, I glimpsed what this midsummer magic might be. In the play within the play in Act V, presented to Theseus, Duke of Athens, on his wedding day, Bottom, the weaver, assumes the role of Pyramus in *Pyramus and Thisbe*. In his comical interpretation of his role, he accidentally gets to the bottom of both plays, *A Midsummer Night's Dream* and *Pyramus and Thisbe* alike. When love and reason are not harmonized by the magic of the mind's executive powers, chaos ensues. Of course, in the play itself, chaos can be magically harmonized. Oberon can send Puck to flit around the world to find the right medicine. Puck's imaginary tricks are meant as a poetic proxy for the real stuff that a healthy mind provides for itself. Indeed, Puck is the power of poetry incarnate, at least as far as a flesh-and-blood actor can so portray him.

An enlightened mind is well orchestrated, brightly optimistic, and grateful, suggests the deep Bottom: "I thank thee, Moon, for shining now so bright. / For by thy gracious, golden, glittering gleams, / I trust to take of truest Thisbe sight."

But Puck's magic is not available to poor Bottom. Disaster soon strikes. A bottomed-out mind dies a comical death. Bottom/Pyramus says the following as he stabs himself, his diction scrambled: "Now am I dead. / Now am I fled. / My soul is in the sky. / Tongue, lose thy light. / Moon, take thy flight."

Indeed, without an enlightened mind, all is jumbled. The tongue loses the light it doesn't possess, and the moon flies from its orderly orbit for no reason.

In rehab, Bottom's buffoonery sent me back to early June 1958, when I took the Pico bus to Santa Monica Beach on a warm Sunday, with *Romeo and Juliet* rolled into my towel. The beach was quiet since few people came before school let out. My plan was to lie in the sun to tan my left-arm's nakedness.

I opened *Romeo*. I read that Juliet "hath not seen the change of fourteen years." She was my age, which I supposed was the reason so many teachers assigned the play in junior high. Her father thought she should wait another two years before getting married, but her mother, Lady Capulet, thought she should marry now. "I was your mother much upon these years / That you are now a maid," she says. "Go, girl, seek happy nights to happy days," says Juliet's nurse.

My mother had shown me none of Lady Capulet's encouragement. Rather, she reminded me on a daily basis of the traps set by wily and trashy girls. Polio was now prevented, but there were new dangers. Delilah was everywhere.

"Look at what Dear Abby says right here," my mother intoned, waving the newspaper. "This eighteen-year-old boy has to marry his sixteen-year-old girlfriend. The girls are supposed to be the ones to look out, but they don't any longer. Do you see that?"

"I'm not getting married."

The last of the morning fog was just burning off at the beach. The end of the pier was still hazy, but it was going to be a beautiful day. A woman and her teenage daughter spread their towels between me and the glittering sea. The girl was my age. The mother was lithe, seemed hardly older than the girl. They stretched out on their backs, already tan for so early in the season. Their breasts were small, shapely, tilted back toward me in an unintended gesture. They sported the same sunglasses, the same shapely tummies. The girl was still. The mother rotated her feet in the sand with a sensuous rhythm that taught me something about the secret crests and crevices of a lean body. Her shoulders just perceptibly followed the rhythm of her feet, and so did the tops of her breasts.

Soon, I was too distracted to read further of Romeo's heat. I had my own problems. I put aside Mercutio's ribald repartee with Romeo about "that very Mab / That plats the manes of horses [read: whores] in the night, / And bakes the elflocks in foul sluttish hairs." Mercutio further explains, "This is the hag, when maids lie on their backs, / That presses them and learns them first to bear." Although at thirteen years old, I was a virgin, I knew what pressing must be, and, from common vernacular, I knew—or thought I knew—what Mercutio's advice about rough sex meant. "If love be rough with you, be rough with love. / Prick love for pricking, and you beat love down."

The particularly seductive Mab lying before me on the beach in Santa Monica, the mother, got up to cool herself in the water. She was hot. The slinky daughter was left alone. I thought that I should say something to her while her mother was dipping her toes. I could test out my freshly contrived easygoing relationship with my less-than-perfect body.

I took off my glasses, got up, and walked toward the water, near the girl.

"Hi," said I, trying not to squint. "Do you want to join your mom for a swim?"

"She's not my mom."

"She looks like you."

"That's what everybody says. She's my dad's new wife."

"Oh. Do you want to swim?"

"I'm afraid of the ocean."

"Come with me, and I'll make sure you don't get into any rough water."

"No, thanks. Try Estelle. She likes the ocean. She likes guys. You're a little young for her, but you never can tell. Tell her I sent you. Tell her—oh, never mind. You're not really her type."

"You don't want to try a swim? The water is calm today."

"I'm afraid of the ocean, calm or not calm."

"Give it a try. Just up to your ankles."

"Forget it. You're not *my* type either."

I swam out toward Estelle. Here was my chance. An older woman. Maybe I was *her* type. She jumped into an oncoming wave, her slender arms above her head, showing her white underarms. Squinting, I caught up with her. The small of her back featured a fine cord of muscle on either side of the pearly bones of her spine. I squinted harder to see her more clearly. She jumped above one wave, then another. With each arch of her back, a widening curve of her white peach bottom showed below the tan line. The water frothed about her, then settled down, running off her glistening skin.

She was a fine fish in the water, lovely in her element. Was this what Lady Capulet meant when she encouraged Juliet about the pleasures of marriage and fruitful sensuality? "The fish lives in the sea, and 'tis much pride / For fair without the fair within to hide." That's what Estelle was, a fish at play, wet and excitable, not as weird as Lady Capulet's image of a fish as sex object, once you saw her for yourself. What fair thing hid under Estelle's bikini bottom?

I said nothing to Estelle as I struggled through the breaking waves, close by her. I dove under the last wave before reaching the calmer water and turned on my back, lying on the golden bosom of the heaving sea.

I did the backstroke languidly in the water's net of reflected sunshine, watching each new pattern of sparkling light form and dissolve. Estelle was on her back too, not far from me but oblivious to my presence. Did she really not see me, or did she just pretend I was not there? It seemed that chance should lead her to a greater distance from me if she really didn't know I was there, so maybe she was staying close just in case she needed help.

Out of the corner of my eye, I saw a large wave and caught it perfectly, shooting forward on its high front. I hoped Estelle was seeing me in my triumph as I kept my head and chest out in front of the wave's curl. Beneath me, the sandy water churned angrily as the undertow broke the rushing energy that carried me shoreward. At the last possible second, I arched up onto my feet, avoiding a face plant in the sand.

Squinting my way back to my towel, I felt better after I found my glasses. Soon, Estelle was back. As she sat on her towel, I noted the symmetrical dimples located just above her gluteal cleft, known as Dimples of Venus, according to the old textbook of human anatomy given to me by my Uncle Jerry, a GP, and husband to my mother's sister, Aunt Frieda, who was older than my mother but said she was younger. Estelle lay back on her towel and turned her feet in the sand. Her stepdaughter remained a sleeping beauty.

Those rotating feet in the warm sand set the hairs on my arms erect. I got up and walked the beach southward, toward Venice Pier, to which I sometimes swam from Santa Monica Pier. Soon, I came to Muscle Beach, the place where men lifted barbells in the sand. In the back of the roped-off area sat a low hut, where a few weightlifters rested in the shade.

A honey-golden man right in front of me shouldered a barbell, ready to squat up and down. Another tan and muscled man lay on his back on a bench with a heavy weight across his chest, pumping it up to the sky. Yet another stood guard at the lifter's head, ready to protect him should the weights fall onto his face. Another honey-colored man stood, wearing a broad leather belt as he dug his elbows into his abdomen, a dumbbell in each upturned hand. He leaned back and bent his elbows up to his chest, grunting, his biceps bulging like melons.

In the hut, a skinny, pale man with red hair and a sunburned nose drank milk from a quart container. He was getting ready. I could see he was in a hurry to become like the others, muscled and honey tan. I felt sorry for him as he poured milk down his throat. Maybe he would always be a runt. He replaced big plates on the bar with little ones.

He asked one of the men, "Can you spot me?"

Next to him, a man was squatting up and down, effortlessly.

He mumbled, "Poor Irish son of a bitch."

I walked back north until I came to a crowd pushing toward an improvised wrestling ring. A barrel of a man was bellowing for challengers. He flexed slabs of muscle on his shoulders and chest, heaved forward a large taut belly, not like the other men at Muscle Beach with their washboard abdomens. He wore a black bikini that curved down under his robust belly.

After some delay, a youngish man with pale skin stepped into the ring. He was well muscled but dwarfed by the Barrel. At first glance, I didn't recognize him, but then I saw he was Preacher Rowe, the most famous high school student in Los Angeles. He rode his motorcycle to the beach and picked fights, always winning. He was known to bite ears; he once bit one clear off. His bullying ways had made him a legend, so it got harder for him to find people who would take him on. Most of the time, Preacher roared away on his bike, without a fight. To his credit, he always looked for somebody his size or bigger. Now he was in the ring with the Barrel, unrecognizable because he seemed so small compared to this behemoth. I guessed he figured he would win based on speed.

He tried to work his quickness to his advantage. He danced around, feinted, and dove under the paws of the bigger man, then jumped back out of reach. He got around behind the Barrel and tried to yank him backward over his extended leg. But the Barrel didn't tip. Rather, he reached over his shoulder and caught Preacher by his scalp. In a flash, he pulled Preacher up over his back and onto his shoulders, grabbed him by the shoulder and hip, and held him up over his head. He turned around slowly with his stunned trophy on high. Then he slammed Preacher into the canvas.

Preacher did not move or speak. The Barrel picked him up and slammed him down again. This time, Preacher bounced a little and moaned. Something in him rallied enough to wave uncle. The Barrel mercifully let him hobble out of the ring. Nobody helped him.

I walked back to my spot on the beach. Estelle was still working her feet in the sand, and her stepdaughter lay still. I still didn't know her name. Suddenly, I no longer cared. I would become a man in my own time and in my own way.

I picked up my towel and book, walked to the bus stop on Pico, and rode the bus back to Beverlywood. I wondered what deity wrote my script, keeping me steadfastly in the same play. God couldn't do all that writing. Besides, it was quite clear that I wasn't always in the same play with the same characters. The other characters kept going off into their own plays. My mother's hurt from her mother's suicide was an old saga, not always intersecting with my story, sometimes taking place in front of me, other times in Winnipeg, or in Kiev, where she was born. And then there were my multiple accidents, not only the milk truck and the wildebeest, but also a host of random events—like the presence on one day of Estelle, her stepdaughter, the Irish runt lifting weights on Muscle Beach, Preacher Rowe, the Barrel, and Romeo—all at play in my mind, almost cohering.

As I progressed in rehab, I could feel my own version of Romeo's fear that some dread "consequence . . . / Shall bitterly begin his fearful date." But Shakespeare draws from English folklore a wider, deeper, and more poetic rendition of fearful fate. Yes, Mab, the queen of sex and aggression, "gallops night by night / Through lovers' brains, and then they dream of love." She also "driveth o'er a soldier's neck, / And then dreams he of cutting foreign throats." But Mab is not all-powerful. She and the primitive drives she represents can be tempered by poetry, as Shakespeare shows us.

The ability to cast Mercutio's Mab and Oberon's Puck into my own chorus gave me more energy to exercise vigorously in the rehab gym and to think creatively. Exercise is obviously necessary to rehabilitate physical injury, but why does artful weaving of one's memories help restore an injured brain? I was a living experiment, a test to help answer this question.

CHAPTER SEVENTEEN

Occupational Therapy

And then I came to understand that I, anyhow, had had plague through all those long years in which, paradoxically enough, I'd believed with all my soul that I was fighting it.

– Albert Camus, *The Plague*, 1948

IN ADDITION TO RECEIVING PHYSICAL AND COGNITIVE THERAPY IN REHAB, I was given a course in occupational therapy. This had nothing to do with my usual occupation. I was taught how to shower, a tricky business since my balance was so poor. I was taught what equipment I would need for my home: a bath bench to protect against further falls, a showerhead that could be brought down to my seated level, and a rubber mat to prevent me from slipping. That I was going to remain disabled was the working assumption.

I was given instructions on how to prepare a grocery list, how to plan meals, and how to make a calendar of chores. I was going to have to take care of myself in a disabled state. My occupational therapist was thus working on my advanced activities of daily living, on my SHAFT: the development of my ability to manage shopping, health care, accounting, food preparation, telephoning and transportation, all independently.

Mixed in with home economics were more cognitive tests. One day after making an omelet on a slanted stove, I was asked to put together a puzzle of the United States, which I did quickly, having done this with my mother when I was five years old. I did not get to a lot of nameless pieces related to Canada and Mexico—not because I couldn't, but because we were out of time.

I was asked to redo the puzzle during our next session. On this occasion, I was given enough time to complete the whole, which was more like a jigsaw puzzle than the usual puzzle of the fifty states, with which I was familiar since the age of five. Did I not have a keloid on my abdomen in the shape of Mexico? I was now told I had improved, having regained some of my ability to operate in new arenas. I didn't believe that I was ever able to do this kind of puzzle any faster, as I was never interested in this kind of thing. And I doubted that my medical colleagues would be any faster than I, for it was unlikely that they possessed my mind's photographic picture of the forty-eight states of the USA in 1949. But, even if I were fast enough, it would be necessary to provide more evidence that I was cognitively fit, said my occupational therapist.

Here is an example of my new occupational challenges, imperfectly recalled now, but remembered well enough to convey the desperation into which I was thrown. I was shown a picture of a wooden base with four slender but sturdy poles reaching upward, each, perhaps, eight inches tall. On each pole in the picture was a stack of small wooden shapes, each with a hole down the middle. Perhaps a broad yellow rectangle was at the bottom of one stack, on which stood a green triangle, then three red balls, and then an unpainted wooden cube. There were four such poles, each stacked randomly. That was the picture. Also in front of me was a real wooden base with colored wooden shapes already arranged on each of four actual poles in a pattern different from those in the picture.

I was asked to recreate the picture by rearranging the shapes already strung before me on the actual poles. But I could move only one piece at a time. If I needed to place a piece to go on the bottom of a specific pole, I had to move pieces one at a time to clear a place for the requisite piece on the correct pole, placing the moved pieces in the strategically best position from which they could be subsequently moved. I soon realized I was copying the arrangement seen on the second pole from the right in the picture on the third actual pole. I couldn't see a quick way to fix this, given the rules. Besides, I was out of time.

It was becoming clear to me that I was not going to be allowed to go back to work until I completed more extensive outpatient rehabilitation, including more puzzles. Five days before I was scheduled to be discharged, Dr. Song, always so supportive, came to my room. This time he surprised me.

He said, "I haven't discussed driving with you. I should have done this earlier. We can't approve your return to driving until you have more outpatient therapy."

I had actually been practicing driving, marching around the corridors with my walker, careful to stop at intersections so as not to be bowled over by a crossing dietary cart. I steered through the hospital restaurant to be sure I could keep track of distracted people looking for a seat while they were carrying trays, or seated diners suddenly pushing their chairs backward into my path. Naively, I thought this adequate drivers' training.

So there it was. I couldn't work. I couldn't drive. And I would have to find somebody to help me shop for the ingredients of any omelet I might want to make.

CHAPTER EIGHTEEN

Afternoon Exercise Class

He's fat, and scant of breath. –
Here, Hamlet, take my napkin, rub thy brows.
The queen carouses to thy fortune, Hamlet.
– William Shakespeare, *Hamlet,* act 5, scene 2

TO SUPPLEMENT MY FORMAL SESSIONS WITH A PHYSICAL THERAPIST EVERY morning, I was offered optional exercise classes in the afternoons. Early on, I was pushed in a wheelchair to the nearby gym, which was cleared for the group activity. Some patients arrived on motorized wheelchairs with straps and headrests.

Others hobbled in with walkers. For each exercise, we were all given our choice of stretchable, color-coded cords. Yellow was easiest, then green, then blue, then red, then black. Nobody chose black.

While remaining seated, we marched through a sequence of stretching the cords on different planes, using different muscles. Each of us was careful not to reinjure whatever was broken. Attempting one exercise, I grasped both ends of my green cord and placed my fists over my sternum, with my elbows fixed against my ribs. I then rotated my forearms to an outstretched position laterally, thus provoking pain in my fractured left collarbone. I was pleased that my ten fractured ribs did not bother me.

As the weeks went by, I was able to use my own hands to wheel my chair to classes. Then I was able to get there with a walker, then with Canadian crutches, then with a cane. I was pleased when I was permitted to navigate back to my room without an escort.

One afternoon, Dr. Kurt Johnson saw me carrying to exercise class a book just given to me for my sixty-seventh birthday, James Shapiro's *Contested Will: Who Wrote Shakespeare?*

Dr. Johnson said, "I would like to read that."

"I will lend it to you when I'm done," I said, trying to picture myself handing over the book as a well-dressed, high-functioning physician, a fantasy that did eventually materialize, though I could not then believe that it would. I was too busy worrying whether I would ever be me, which dovetailed with my longstanding thoughts about whether Shakespeare was really Shakespeare.

In an essay at the end of his thorough book, Professor Shapiro argues that William Shakespeare of Stratford-upon-Avon indeed wrote the plays we attribute to him. Earlier in the book, he demolishes the many attempts to find another author for the famous plays. And in the book's conclusion, he shows that surviving rehearsal copies of some of the plays contain an actor's name, not the name of the character he is playing, thus revealing an awareness of theater business that candidates for the "real Shakespeare," like the Earl of Oxford or Sir Francis Bacon, would not possess. But what if Bacon gave a crafted play to Shakespeare, who then copied it into a form useful for production?

Dr. Johnson reminded me why I doubted that rural Will, with a provincial education in Stratford, wrote the renowned plays. *Coriolanus* was Shakespeare's best portrayal of a man whose executive function is risible. This was my problem in rehab, so this play was exercising my mind, even as I stretched the green cords. What could a glove maker's son in Stratford know about a risible executive function?

Shakespeare focuses on Coriolanus's failure of perspicacity, his inability to do the right thing at the right time, every scene contributing to the portrayal of this great warrior's consistently inappropriate behavior. Perhaps this is why T. S. Eliot thought *Coriolanus* to be "Shakespeare's finest artistic achievement in tragedy." But how did the bard know so much about impoverished executive function when no one else did?

I wanted to believe that my knowledge about Shakespeare proved that my accident had not undone my capacity to think. But this was not an easy go. I kept circling back to the fact that in Africa, I had crashed into the inevitable consequences of the Ides of August. No exercise class was likely to undo this crash. The tragedies of Caesar and Coriolanus cannot be undone.

CHAPTER
NINTEEN
The Patient as Monster

Now see that noble and most sovereign reason
Like sweet bells jangled, out of tune and harsh;
That unmatched form and feature of blown youth
Blasted with ecstasy.

– William Shakespeare, *Hamlet,* act 3, scene 1

UNBEKNOWNST TO MY CAREGIVERS, I RUMINATED ON THE WAYS I WAS A monster. Most of my therapists thought me to be kind, polite, and blessed by many friends, some of whom visited me almost nightly. But my mind roiled.

I knew from my old memories how bad accidents produce

deformities of body and mind. I knew that because I was accident-prone, deaf in my left ear, and cross-eyed with a crippled left arm, and l had to be displayed to the principal of Castle Heights Elementary and her cohorts from the Los Angeles Board of Education—and, unsurprisingly, I was now, again, on display, this time daily, with a jammed mind and a shattered pelvis. What remained was my dogged determination to master trauma and not to sink into the Slough of Despond, where wasteful self-pity prevailed.

I thought much of *The Tempest*'s Prospero, the all-powerful magician who overcomes his losses. His role as the Duke of Milan was filched from him by his ambitious brother, who took advantage of Prospero's withdrawal from ruling his duchy, so that he might master the occult knowledge in those precious books that he brought with him into exile, a bookish man like me.

Prospero and his daughter are set adrift on the open sea, miraculously surviving a voyage designed to be fatal. He then magically establishes himself on a strange island. The physical location of the island is unclear, but it seems to be someplace in the Mediterranean, as the doomed ship at the play's opening is said to be sailing from Tunis to Naples. But the actual geography of the Mediterranean is not the geography that Shakespeare has in mind, for here and everywhere in his work, he tracks the topography of the mind itself.

On Prospero's island, the mind's monstrous id is represented by Caliban, "a savage and deformed slave," "a freckled whelp, hag-born, not honour'd with / A human shape." In the role of the unrestrained id, Caliban intends to rape Miranda, Prospero's daughter. "Thou didst seek to violate / The honor of my child," Prospero reminds the slave. "Would't it been done," barks Caliban. "Thou didst prevent me; I had peopled else / This isle with Calibans." Miranda adds that Caliban stems from a "vile race," the offspring of the witch Sycorax and the devil.

Prospero is able to prevent the rape of his daughter because he is the master of this island, if not of his lost duchy of Milan. Because the island is his mind, and he has acquired the necessary magic to master his mental arena, it matters little that he was never master of his duchy. Magic manipulation does not work out in the world, but it can work in the web of the mind. Just as a man's subconscious can arrange anything in his dreams, Prospero, with his artful magic, can control not only cognitive learning (he is still in possession of his library), but also others' morality. He is the most perfect example of an idealized superego, beyond anything that Freud could have imagined. He uses his "art" to orchestrate the storm that brings his enemies into a realm where their faults and failures fade away and their minds are mended.

As Prospero directs artful magic via the dreamlike flitting of Ariel, what we see enacted on stage is the re-harmonization of the human mind's propensity for mayhem. Ariel, like Puck in *A Midsummer Night's Dream,* is the objective correlative of an artful executive function, the poetry of the mind, the power to tune the current music. In Act I, scene ii, he sings a famous lyric that nullifies even death, elevating it into a larger harmony:

> Full fathom five thy father lies;
> Of his bones are coral made;
> Those are pearls that were his eyes:

Nothing of him that doth fade,
But doth suffer a sea-change
Into something rich and strange.
Sea-nymphs hourly sing his knell:
Hark! Now I hear them—Ding-dong bell.

The well-composed mind is indeed "rich and strange," terms that would likely suggest to an Elizabethan audience the Christian resurrection and eternal life. But Shakespeare means no such thing. Rather, Ariel offers a poet's alternative to messianic redemption. The artful orchestration of the mind's full capacities lies not in coral or material eyeballs, but in the power of the pearls of poetry. It is precisely poetry that makes possible "a sea-change / Into something rich and strange," pearls into poetry, and poetry into renewal. This is the "bell" that Ariel rings.

And here I was, polite as could be, a gentleman, putting on a good face so that nobody would suspect that I feared myself a monster, a deformed slave, a man crippled one too many times, misshapen, a Caliban, a man of broken bones and broken spirit, whom even Ariel and Puck could not put back together again.

CHAPTER

TWENTY

Preparing for Outpatient Therapy

You would play upon me. You would seem to know my stops. You would pluck out the heart of my mystery. You would sound me from my lowest note to the top of my compass. And there is music, excellent voice, in this little organ [recorder], yet cannot you make it speak? 'Sblood, do you think I am easier to be played on than a pipe?

– William Shakespeare, *Hamlet,* act 3, scene 2

WITH MY DISCHARGE TO OUTPATIENT THERAPY EXPECTED SOON, DR. Kurt Johnson went over with me some preliminary cognitive testing. One of these practice tests particularly irked me, probably because it, a simple task, was humiliatingly difficult. And it convinced Dr. Johnson that Dr. Song was correct: I should not drive, "for now." This proclamation came quietly, as if it were not devastating.

I was given sheets of paper with long rows of intermixed letters and numerals. I was told to place a diagonal line through all the twos and sevens as fast as I could. My livelihood rode on lines of numbers and letters, all in small print.

I judged it useless to point out that since I lacked binocular vision, I would have to use one eye at a time to isolate each and every symbol to make sure that I did not confuse capital T's for sevens, or capital Z's for twos. I had long been a thoughtful reader, but never a rapid reader, and I cringed at using my experience as a literary critic to cross out twos and sevens. As an undergraduate at Berkeley, I learned the futility of trying to quicken my reading by using Evelyn Wood's program for speed-reading. My eyes didn't work that way. This past medical history regarding my eyes was too tedious to explain to Dr. Kurt Johnson, too likely to make me sound like a verbose, brain-injured patient.

On each trial of this vexing exercise, I could tell that I wasn't going fast enough to pass. I started to go faster, unsure about my accuracy in distinguishing T's from sevens and Z's from twos. I didn't pass. And I therefore couldn't drive.

Dr. Johnson kindly but very seriously alerted me, "Next time, remember that accuracy is more important than speed."

"Do you have evidence that correlates this test of twos and sevens with safe driving?"

He answered, "We argue about that."

I wanted to push this lack of data to my advantage, but I checked myself, knowing how quickly I would become tiresome.

But I did ask, "Am I ever going to go back to work?"

"I am not a betting man, but if I had to bet, I would bet on yes."

"When?"

"I don't know, but I'm still thinking about February, late February."

I had been hoping for February 1, so I figured the possibility of going back to work might still be good.

CHAPTER TWENTY-ONE

Weekly Assessments

I would not even suppress my suspicion, held on psychological grounds, that I actually seek digressions and circumlocutions, or at least welcome with alacrity any occasion for such, because I am afraid of what is coming.

– Thomas Mann, *Doctor Faustus*

EVERY WEEK THE ENTIRE REHAB TEAM MET IN A WINDOWLESS, CAVE-LIKE room around a collection of tables pushed together. One by one, patients were brought in for a brief summary of progress. Each patient arrived a few moments before his or her appointment and waited in the hallway. Because of the severity of my injuries, I had to miss my first few meetings, but I was eventually brought in a wheelchair to wait my turn.

In the cave, I heard reports from various therapists, who made me think they were talking about somebody else. "He is now ordering his own meals." "He no longer requires a constant companion." "He reads recreationally." "He has not fallen." "He is now walking with a walker." "He has come here today without an escort."

The meeting never seemed to be about me, for these reports about the patient's progress must certainly be about somebody else. I found it easy to heed Vicky's warning to listen quietly and not say too much. Why would I have an opinion about other patients? And it so happened on the occasion of my last meeting in the cave that Vicky was the one who came out to the hallway to invite me in.

She repeated, "Remember, don't talk too much."

So, I said little. I was chained in Plato's famous cave, unable to turn, forced to stare at the blank wall in front me, barely lit by light coming from the cave opening, until humanlike shadows appeared, perhaps cast by the light coming from behind me. Did the shadows represent me, the people sitting in front of me, or other people behind me?

Vicky said, "This week, Dr. Erlich walked with his cane out of the hospital, across Pacific Avenue, and onto the campus. We got to Drumheller Fountain, walked around it, and came back, all without needing a break."

That was true. I recalled how determined I was to walk well on my first venture outdoors in a long time. Exhilarated, I was soon fighting fatigue as we crossed the Burke-Gilman bike trail, where I had ridden many a time. I was sure to check for oncoming bike traffic, fatigued but careful. That walk and that fatigue suddenly felt real. And the team of therapists suddenly consisted of real people. I, too, was more than a shadow. I had made real progress.

Yet I was stunned when Dr. Kurt Johnson said, "We think you are close to going home. We're planning for Wednesday, November 9th. In the morning."

I said, "I'm getting better faster here than I would at home."

Vicky said, "Most patients who are ready to go home feel that way."

That afternoon, I walked on my own to the scheduled class for chair exercises, but I didn't take a seat. Rather, I stood, watching the only patient, a tall, slender young man who had arrived in a complex wheelchair, accompanied by his attendant. His head was fixed in a halo, a contraption that circled his head and extended down the back of his neck, propping up his head. In addition, narrow rods reached down laterally from the sides of a headband to rest on shoulder pads. He had likely broken his neck in a bad fall from a height or a motorcycle accident. His attendant stood to one side as he stretched a yellow rubber cord. He grasped the ends of the cord with both hands, but he quickly gave up, fatigued.

I returned to my room to read *The New England Journal of Medicine*. I couldn't focus, ruminating instead on the Cave of Assessment. I was assessed to be ready for discharge. Was I not lucky? The young man in his halo contraption, so badly injured, would not likely go home, but I was Defoe's Robinson Crusoe, with a Man Friday built into my being. With my internalized Friday, a creative chap, I was to be rescued from my island of wreckage. The boy in the halo, I feared, would remain marooned.

CHAPTER TWENTY-TWO

Dickie's Spider Bite, Age Fifteen

There may be in the cup
A spider steep'd, and one may drink. . . .
But if one present
The abhorr'd ingredient to his eye, make known
How he hath drunk, he cracks his gorge, his sides,
With violent hefts. I have drunk and seen the spider.
– William Shakespeare, *The Winter's Tale,* act 2, scene 1

BUT WHO SAID THAT I MYSELF WAS NOT MAROONED? WAS NOT MY friend Dickie thought to have suffered a spider bite from which he would recover? Instead, he died of leukemia before he'd turned sixteen.

In rehab, I recalled my mother talking on the phone with Dickie's mother, Rosie, speaking with her contrived "calm" voice, which was not nearly as reassuring as she intended it to be. She did not have the gift of projecting confidence in a good outcome, and her attempts to do so usually produced the opposite effect. Her own trauma in early life rippled through her reassurance.

"I'm sure it's nothing," she said to Rosie. "My Vickie-Boy has had things like that."

That evening she came to say good night to me as I was getting into bed, which was now in the living room, because we were adding three small bedrooms and a bath upstairs. For a reason that I could not fathom at the time, my mother found it urgent to tell me that Red Skelton, the famous comedian, was taking his son around the world because the doctors could do no more for him. He was dying of leukemia, she said.

And then she said, with a pseudo casualness that terrified me, "And you know somebody with leukemia. Would you like to know who it is?"

"No," I whispered, thinking it was me.

After my grandfather—my *Zadie*—had another heart attack, my father took me to visit him at Cedars of Lebanon Hospital. Mixed in with this memory of my zadie is my memory of Dickie lying in the same hospital. Zadie was recovering from a heart attack, and Dickie was supposedly recovering from a spider bite, for that is what his parents told him and what my mother told me. Nobody, including Dickie, ever saw the spider. So gentle, clever, and funny, Dickie would be OK.

Dickie's easygoing parents didn't worry about the bombing of Pearl Harbor, or the Battle of the Bulge, or the Holocaust, very different from my mother, who primed me from the time I was a toddler with the urgency of these subjects. Frankie and Rosie, true to their upbeat names, had a swimming pool in their backyard in Burbank, where they had moved from Venice to get away from the war veterans and their memories.

A cinder-block wall stood about five feet high, three feet back from the deep end of the pool. Dickie and I liked to dive off that wall, mainly because we were forbidden to do so. I knew what terrible things might happen if I dove and missed, but I dove anyway, because Dickie made it seem safe. And it was.

"Don't smash your brains out," he would say, jackknifing into the water.

In the hospital, Dickie was put on a strict diet. I smuggled in hamburgers when he begged me to do so.

Lying in a mechanized bed, he told me a joke about a kid who had a condom demonstrated to him on a cucumber: "The kid said to his teacher, 'Of course, you wouldn't make a baby if you used a cucumber.'"

He added, "What do you get if you cross a melon with Lassie?"

"I don't know," I said.

"A melon-collie baby," he crooned.

I envied him, because he was smart and carried a tune. I laughed at his joke, but I was terrified by his paleness. This was some spider bite.

Frankie came in, also pale. He wore a fake smile.

"Do you know that you were born in this hospital, Cedars of Lebanon?" Frankie asked. He had fat jowls and yellow fat pads under his eyes. "Would you like to come downstairs and have dinner with me? I'm famished. Haven't eaten all day."

“I’m hungry too,” I answered, already worried.

“Just after you were born, I visited your mom here. Your dad was in Texas, in boot camp. He didn’t get to see you until a few weeks later. They gave him enough leave to take the train, see you for a day, and take the train back. Dickie was born here just three weeks before. I was lucky they hadn’t sent me to the Pacific yet. A lot of boys died out there.”

I pressed him about the nature of spider bites. My self-inflicted dullness was failing. Frankie was worn out. A spider bite wouldn’t do that.

I said, “I saw this program on Gila monsters that bite you, and sometimes you die. But if you don’t die, you’re fine after a while. They also showed spiders and tarantulas. Same thing. Some spiders give you sores that never heal. They inject a poison that eats away at your foot or whatever they bite, and that leaves a big hole, but you can get that fixed if—”

“Do you know what’s really wrong with Dickie?”

“No,” I said dumbly.

“Your parents never told you?”

“No.”

The facts were forthcoming. By putting two and two together, I knew what they would be, considering the yellow pads under Frankie’s eyes and my mother sitting by my bed and telling me, for a reason I was supposed to guess, about Red Skelton’s son. But Frankie had to present the facts to me.

“I’d guessed they wouldn’t. Dickie’s got leukemia. He’s going to die.”

He didn’t cry, but it looked like he was going to.

"Excuse me," he said. "I have to go. My amebic dysentery is kicking up."

Frankie came back from the bathroom wiping his face with a hankie. He and my father always carried a hankie, and my father tried to get me to carry one too. Both my grandfathers had summer hats and winter hats, and my father had year-round hankies. So did Frankie. I never wore a hat or carried a hankie.

He started talking about his dysentery in a humorous way, as he always did. There is something funny about diarrhea, and Frankie made it even funnier.

"I got it in the Pacific, fighting the Japanese. Because of that, I got disability from Uncle Sam, enough so I could stop selling shoes for my father-in-law. With the dough, I went to law school. The Japanese bombed Pearl Harbor so I could go to the Pacific and get a bug up my ass so the government would pay my way to law school—when they goddamn got around to paying—so I could get this crazy Japanese client of mine off when he got caught driving drunk on the Fourth of July . . . the Fourth of July, for God's sake! Go figure. Go figure. A drunk Jap on the Fourth."

I knew about the true nature of Dickie's condition the whole time although I silently denied it, because that is what minds do.

During his last hospitalization, Dickie again asked me to smuggle in hamburgers. We had a good meal, with fries dipped in ketchup squeezed from packets, and then he dozed off. As he slept, I studied tenth-grade biology. A nurse came in and took his temperature, awakening him. She chastised him for eating nothing, and we laughed because right there in the wastebasket were signs of the contraband. Nobody had told him he was dying.

Suddenly, he grew serious. "I found a hospital bill in the house. You know, a statement. It said I have leukemia. But my father brought a doctor over to explain that it was a mistake. He said they classify spider bites the same way as leukemia for billing purposes. Do you believe that?"

"I don't know."

"But what do you think?"

"I'm not a doctor. It's hard to know what to think."

"Well, I know what you would think if you found the bill. You would think you had leukemia."

"You know, for the oddest reason, I've been thinking I *do* have leukemia. Something my mother said about Red Skelton's son made me worry. Then I got a rash on my groin, and that, along with what my mother said, made me think I had leukemia. My mother says strange things. She's an orphan."

"My mother smiles all the time," Dickie said. "She says it's no good to think too much."

A few days later, Dickie went home. I called his house, hoping he forgot about that bill. Frankie answered. He sounded drunk. He said I couldn't talk to Dickie.

"We had a bad night last night. Dickie had to move his bowels but he couldn't. He couldn't get it out. He was so constipated, he was crying. Finally, I had to put my finger up there and pull it out. Now he's asleep. I can't wake him now. I don't have the heart."

A day or two later, on a school morning, the phone rang as I was on my way out the door to my biology examination. My mother answered. I waited at the front door, I knew not why.

My mother called me back to her bedroom.

"Dickie passed away in his sleep. He didn't suffer. But oh my God, they never told him. Last night they showed home movies from when they lived at the beach, and then he died in his sleep. They never told him."

At Dickie's funeral, I was sickened to see rouge on his cheeks, his casket obscenely open. There were no seats in the chapel in the Jewish part of Forest Lawn, so my father and I stood outside around loudspeakers with a crowd of high school students from Burbank. My father somehow knew how to get me inside. He marched me past the ushers who tried to stop him but then changed their minds. He ushered me to the back of the chapel, where we stood. The casket was light gray and chrome, padded inside with white satin.

Dickie Salter, age nine

On the way back to the car with my parents, walking carefully on the grass between flat grave markers, I felt an insect crawl up my leg. I stopped, pulled up my pant leg, and pulled out the black bug with its wriggling legs. I thought it was a spider, but it was a beetle, and I sobbed. My father put his arm around me, something he usually wouldn't do. Things weren't always what they seemed. My father loved me, and I didn't have leukemia. But Dickie, born on October 4, 1944 and dead on June 6, 1960—never sure what had hit him but doubting it was a spider—was now clad in satin for eternity.

Maybe I was like him, writhing in rehab, still unsure whether I was living or dying. I fretted quietly about what I wasn't being told. Dickie hadn't been told he was dying. I hadn't been told that I would never function well enough to work.

CHAPTER TWENTY-THREE

Outpatient

What is infirm from your sound parts shall fly,
Health shall live free and sickness freely die.

– William Shakespeare,
All's Well That Ends Well, act 2, scene 1

AFTER I PROVED TO MY OCCUPATIONAL THERAPIST THAT I COULD MAKE an omelet, that I could dice a tomato, grate cheese, and turn the eggs over just so on a problematically slanted stove, I was scheduled to be discharged from Eight East. I was reading medical journals, talking, and walking.

My sister, Nan, agreed to come from Los Angeles to help me at home. And Denise came to join Nan. A former employee of mine, then working for another physician, she quit her job to come live in my house, to help with shopping, cooking, cleaning, all of the little chores I used to do for myself. Suddenly overwhelmed by my neediness, I realized that I had never bothered being grateful for independence and autonomy, neither of which were present in the hospital, and neither of which would be present at home, at least for now. Denise would drive me to my rehab appointments, both physical and cognitive.

My mood, often despondent but sometimes surprisingly upbeat while I was in the hospital, darkened decidedly on arriving home. Able to sleep in my own bed for the first time in three months, I slept well. But I was always sleepy—in bed by 7:30 in the evening and often not able to get up until 11:00 a.m.

Denise had to force me out of bed: "Your breakfast is ready. Eggs and toast, with butter."

She would then insist that I go to the gym, "or you'll never get better."

I made progress at a turtle's pace, becoming more and more fearful that I would never drive or work again. I repeated these worries to visiting friends until they begged me to stop.

"Don't forget," Marie-Louise would say kindly, "You're trying to be less wordy and less repetitive so you won't sound brain injured."

It did not help when my therapists told me over and again that all brain-injured patients find being home more exhausting than the pervasive care and commotion of the hospital.

Denise drove me to my old gym. The manager let me renew my membership at a reduced rate. Denise stood by my side, holding my cane, making sure I didn't fall when I balanced myself on one foot while standing on the large half-ball. She helped me stretch, which was still a surprising challenge for me. Able to exercise alone for a bit, I was reminded of myself as a young father committed to providing my children with the kind of loving care I would have wanted myself as a child. In raising my children, I fathered myself. I was doing that again.

Just after Denise drove me home, Dr. Kurt Johnson called.

He said, "We just had a team meeting. I discovered that you were sent home with no outpatient program for three weeks. I read them the riot act. I said, 'You gave him physical therapy seven days a week while he was in the hospital, and you sent him home with nothing? You have him set up for cognitive therapy in three weeks, and he was admitted here, to the brain injury program?' We talked about that. Can you come in today so we can fix it?"

Dr. Johnson suggested two o'clock. I was there on time, chauffeured by Denise.

Dr. Johnson repeated what he'd told me when he'd first introduced himself, saying, "It is an honor to work with you."

Not many people can say such a thing with sincerity, but Dr. Kurt Johnson could.

He added, "I have spoken with Dr. Bell about you. As you know, she is the chairman of the department and runs the brain injury clinic. She is interested in your case. She is going to arrange for you to attend her clinic as an observer. This will take a little doing, but it should be a good opportunity for you. This is a large institution, and we have to get formal permission for you to observe in a university clinic."

This opportunity sounded promising, allowing me to believe that I might work again. But first I had to go back to cooking classes and word puzzles.

Then came more serious challenges.

CHAPTER TWENTY-FOUR

Cognitive Testing

It's admitted on all sides that medical men aren't now what they used to be. They used to be talented, observing, educated men. But now any whipper- snapper out of an apothecary's shop can call himself a doctor. I believe no kind of education is now thought necessary.

– Anthony Trollope, *Barchester Towers*

WHILE I FIDGETED IN THE PATIENTS' WAITING AREA, EAGER FOR JANE to call me in for my scheduled full day of cognitive testing, an attractive blonde, not much younger than I, happened to sit down next to me. Kitty-corner from her was a young man, presumably her son, perhaps eighteen to twenty years old, seated in a wheelchair, his head in a helmet, his posture suggesting spinal cord damage. I asked the woman her name.

"Chris," she said with a lovely smile.

"What brings you here today?" I asked in my kindest voice.

"Jimmy's getting cognitive testing. I am looking for a miracle. We are not giving up hope. More than a year ago, we sent Jimmy off to college at Western. He's such a bright young man. Early on in his first semester, he had a party in his dorm room. I think there was a lot of alcohol. A friend of his asked him if he wanted to try some drug. I think it was morphine. Jimmy went to sleep on the floor, and everybody went home. He didn't wake up for more than twenty-four hours. His friends finally realized that they hadn't seen him for a while. They found him unconscious, and he was put on a breathing machine. At Harborview Hospital, they did an MRI. They told us he had severe injury to both sides of his brain from lack of oxygen. They asked if we wanted to stop the breathing machine, as his outcome was not going to be good. We said absolutely not. And we're still waiting for a miracle. Jimmy is improving. He's a smart boy."

Just as Chris came to a pause in her story of severe brain injury, Jane called my name, pulling me out of reverie. I was busy reminding myself that I couldn't be as brain injured as this young man, that I was still man enough to find Chris attractive and be ashamed about it, and that I, like Chris, still had the capacity to be a good parent.

Jane quickly got down to business with a string of brief questions, some of which were bizarrely simple, like, "Define apple." Her questions continued in the same vein, like, "What is water?" These questions seemed oddly chosen for somebody who is supposed to be educated. "On what continent is the Sahara Desert?" I wondered, how brain injured do they think I am? I may be stupid enough to fall off a bike in Africa, but I certainly know where Africa's Sahara Desert is and what water is. To which of the advanced activities of daily living did these questions pertain? I never give this kind of testing in my practice, so I couldn't tell which of my cognitive abilities were being tested. This made me nervous.

While answering the question about the definition of water, I shot off my mouth: "Water is H2O, two molecules of standard hydrogen and one molecule of standard oxygen. But you can also have various forms of heavy water, which include deuterium and tritium, or even oxygen-18 instead of oxygen-16." I couldn't remember why exactly these were important, but that didn't stop me.

Jane wrote down much of my dissertation.

"Let's try something easier," smiled Jane. "While we are talking about water, what is its boiling temperature?"

That was indeed easy. But soon I was in a panic. I have rarely been one to draw a blank, but there I was, so brain-injured, or so fearful of being thought brain-injured, that I had no idea of the temperature at which water boils.

In the nick of time, I uttered, "One hundred degrees Centigrade." I did not know where that came from, and I surprised myself by adding, "Two hundred twelve degrees Fahrenheit." Of course I knew that, but for a moment, these facts had gone AOL.

The neurochemistry of memory retrieval is, in fact, poorly understood. What neurons are jarred when a bright but anxious college student draws a blank on a final examination? What exactly happened in my brain when I was asked about the boiling temperature of water? What precisely was jarred on the wildebeest crossing in Kenya?

I could see that Jane was setting up another task, so I settled myself down. She got out a deck of small cards and told me that I would have to sort them according to a plan she would give me.

I knew the Wisconsin Card Sorting Test was a way to evaluate a patient's executive function, for it was frequently mentioned in the Methods section of scholarly papers on cognitive aspects of, say, Alzheimer's disease, but I had never seen it, and I had no idea how it worked. As Jane explained what I was to do, I realized that this must be it. She laid out four cards. I saw that the cards were arranged so that the first had two red triangles; the second one, a yellow star; the third, four blue diamonds; the fourth, three green discs. Four numbers, four shapes, four colors. That would make three categories to go with four cards. That seemed clear, 1-2-3-4, but I was already anxious, certain that the point of the test was not to see if I could count to four.

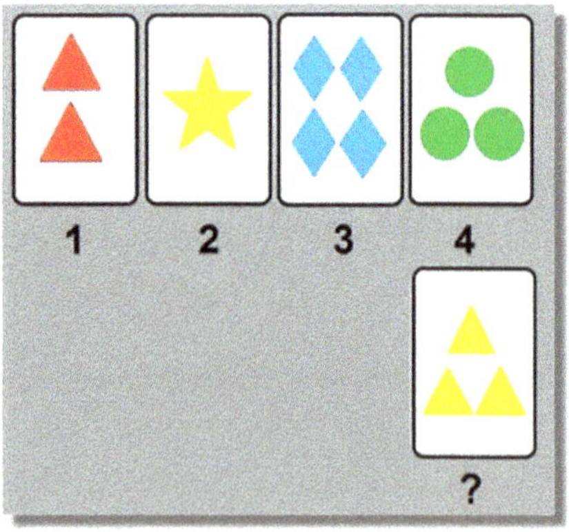

As she handed me the deck, kind Jane said, "Now you start sorting these cards. Place each card, one at a time, on the table just below one of the four sample cards, as in solitaire, choosing the category in which each card belongs. I'll let you know if you make a mistake."

"How do I know what category you have decided is correct?"

"That is for you to decide."

Damn it, I thought, *more random bullshit, and she'll change the rules as we go. Well,* I continued to myself, *there are three categories: number, color, and shape.* Just in case I might need these three categories ready at hand, I quickly invented a mnemonic: North Carolina State. I would begin categorizing by North—that is, by number—placing three yellow triangles below the three green discs, mindful that I might need to change gears.

"Incorrect," intoned Jane.

So I turned to categorizing by Carolina—that is, by color.

"Correct."

I kept going with color until I ran out of cards.

"What now?" I asked politely.

Jane provided another deck, and I kept going by color.

"Incorrect."

I suspected that she'd let me run out of cards so I might lose track of where I was, but I was ready. North Carolina *State.*

"I'm going to sort by shape," said I. And I did.

"Correct," she said. "And we can stop here because you obviously know what you're doing. We can go on to another task. Tell me those twelve words I asked you to remember a little while ago."

I was ready with another of my mnemonic tricks. I had put Jane's twelve random objects into a visual form, a scene. That was on February 15, 2012. I still have a picture in my mind of Coriolanus, a man who "throws without distinction," standing at the head of a street, throwing something toward a beef steer who was stopped in his tracks by a snake. The snake had paused before a hole dug in the road, beyond which lay an old-fashioned film canister, with the name of the film written on its edge: "Discrete." Beyond the film canister, in the middle of the street, sat a potted lily and a tin helmet. To this day, my well-visualized scene contains ten objects, the other two having vanished into the dead holes of my brain's blanks. This is a rough facsimile of my invented scene:

With the scene in mind, I rattled off, "Throw, Street, Beef, Snake, Dug, Film, Discrete, Lily, Helmet, Tin." Able to recall these ten and the two others (but what *did* Coriolanus throw?), I thought that I might yet go back to work.

I have no way of knowing whether Jane meant *discrete*, meaning "distinct," or *discreet*, meaning "discerning," but I doubt that I was then sufficiently discerning to explain the distinction.

Jane then produced a small keypad, like one from an old telegraph office. She asked me to tap as fast as I could with my right index finger, my wrist held just so.

She said, “You must push the lever all the way down and let it come all the way up; otherwise, it won’t count. But go as fast as you can.”

Dr. Kurt Johnson had alerted me that in cognitive testing, accuracy trumped speed. So I tapped out a nonexistent Morse code as fast as I could while remaining accurate.

I did about fifty in about fifteen seconds, during five sets, and then Jane said, “Stop. Let’s go on to your left hand.”

She wanted me to turn my left wrist just so, but I had to explain to her that since my childhood accident, I couldn’t supinate my left palm. She had a job to do and kept urging me to place my wrist differently, despite my request for mercy. But she had a kind heart, and soon she let me be comfortable. Having made no errors with my right hand, I tapped my left index finger with more authority, matching the speed and accuracy of my right hand. I was pleased, but I had no idea how fast I was supposed to go.

When I asked, Jane answered, “You did OK.”

She then announced, “I want you to follow me as I give you an example of the next task. The idea is to look at a set of pictures on the computer screen and tell me what number is being suggested. For instance, what number is suggested by this?”

She showed me a picture of a squiggly Roman numeral IV. I have devoted my intellectual life—first as a professor of literature, and later as a neurologist—to literacy and numeracy. Numerals are not the same as numbers. Numerals do not suggest numbers. They do not suggest anything. Rather, they represent numbers in a defined and fixed way. We can change the definition of how numbers are represented. We now agree that Arabic numerals are what we use to represent numbers, thus abandoning Roman numerals. Numerals are symbols. Numbers are not symbols, but abstractions. And what they abstract is a specific sum of something actually counted. The Roman numeral *IV* and the Arabic numeral *4* symbolize the number four, which means an abstraction of any four objects that can be counted reliably. No symbol *suggests*. The + symbol does not *suggest* addition, but unambiguously defines a specific action in arithmetic. Suggestion comes from the world of poetry and art. Mixing numeracy and literacy so casually drove me to distraction. And matters got worse.

Jane then showed me more complicated pictures that were supposed to suggest "either the number one, the number two, the number three, or the number four." How difficult could this be? It must be some analogue to the Wisconsin Card Sorting Test, with its four initial cards. Now I had four numbers to assign. All I needed to do was figure out the categories in which I was to count. Gregor Mendel founded modern genetics by using an essential scientific tool. He counted carefully. For each of twenty-nine thousand generations of hybridized peas, he recorded the exact number of yellow and green offspring. Nobody ever thought to do this before. But what was I supposed to count? I soon learned that I couldn't find an analogue to North Carolina State.

Because I have no examples of this test and do not even know its name, I am going to use, as a proxy for what I was shown, a lithograph by Alexander Calder, for this is what the pictures I did see actually recalled to me. I still own a few of Calder's lithographs. In graduate school at Berkeley, I supported myself by selling Calder's lithos, which I had purchased in Paris.

The pictures that earnest Jane showed me were not different in general appearance and ambiguity. What number does this lithograph suggest? Could it be *one*, as there is one uniquely colored disc, a standout red? Could it be *two*, as there are repeated sets of two: two black discs in the upper left corner, two in the lower right corner, and two black spirals center stage? Might the number suggested be *three*, given that there are three "sets," or three kinds of objects, black disc, red disc, and spirals? Or might the suggested number be *four*, with the objects to be counted being the most common ones, the four black discs?

Could the test designer, who thinks that numerals suggest numbers, have in mind the sophisticated idea of counting "sets" as a way of getting to a "suggested" number? I now suspect that this was possibly one of the "correct" strategies, with other strategies to be chosen after an initial trial was rejected, just as in the world of North Carolina State. I now think that I was supposed to keep trying strategy after strategy until I hit on one that Jane would brand as "correct," then stick with that until she said, "Incorrect." But I was in no mood to make inane guesses.

"Damn it, none of the above."

Jane saw the state I was in, and it wasn't North Carolina, Wisconsin, or rotten Denmark. She stopped the exercise, which, she said, was added at the last minute, I suppose just for me, without anyone realizing the stench it would make in my mind. The specialists in cognitive testing to whom I refer tell me that their tests have built-in corrections for emotional factors, so maybe I was more brain injured than overwrought by the jumble of numeracy and literacy.

I soon met with Dr. Pepping and my "team" to go over the test results. I learned that I got the highest score they ever gave on their general knowledge test. That was the good news. I learned that on what I called "the telegraph test," I was in the thirty-fifth percentile with my right hand and the sixty-fifth percentile with my left hand. My left hand was actually better despite the crippling from being run over by a milk truck. This made me worry that my team would judge my left hemisphere to be particularly injured, for it had just run my right hand into that rather low percentile. It would not help me to remind the team that I was following Dr. Johnson's warning to be accurate rather than fast, especially when using my right hand. I was terrified that I had telegraphed myself to hell.

Referring to these results, Dr. Pepping said brightly, "I don't think we have to make anything about the speed of Dr. Erlich's tapping."

I learned that Jane stopped the "Calder" test because I was so angry, not because I was frustrated. And this was a problem too. I apologized for offending Jane, if that was what I'd done, and then I tried to explain how my background made this test insufferable.

"Don't you think anything is wrong with you?" I was asked.

I understood that I had just committed the cardinal error of a brain-injured patient. I had implied that I didn't believe that I was brain injured, and that meant I still was. Damn numeracy, damn literacy, and damn Alexander Calder. Damn the four playing cards and damn my imaginary four auxiliary mansions at the equally imaginary hospital in Detroit.

As I recount this meeting with Dr. Pepping, I see that I am now so busy proving how clever I am that I am not capturing how I must have appeared then. Dr. Pepping concluded the meeting by telling me that I could not drive or go back to work until I proved myself cognitively and emotionally more competent.

CHAPTER TWENTY-FIVE

The Slab of Granite Crawls

This is an art
Which does mend nature – change it rather, but
The art itself is nature.
– William Shakespeare, *The Winter's Tale,* act 4, scene 4

I recall another morning at home, waking to Denise's urging me to eat my breakfast "already." Obediently, I ate and got into my car, allowing Denise to chauffer me to the UW for more physical therapy. There, more awake, I walked to the elevator, carrying my cane ostentatiously, not using it. I rode to the eighth floor, where I checked in, as usual. I waited patiently to be called into my appointment with Ashley Nicole Dennis, who was substituting for Vicky. Ashley would apply her new regimen of stretching me forcefully. I liked to call her by her initials, AND, for that is how her name appeared on my schedule, and she reliably added something more, just when I'd thought we were done.

Chris walked into the waiting area with Jimmy in his wheelchair. She sat down opposite me, parking her son next to her. He was struggling to get out of his jacket, a task that was clearly beyond him. His mother watched him carefully in the way she probably watched him take his first steps. Worried that he would soon propel himself out of the chair, she asked him sweetly if he needed help, which she promptly offered. The two smiled at each other, much as I myself had exchanged smiles with my own children.

AND interrupted my memories.

"Are you ready?" she smiled.

I was.

As expected, she was particularly aggressive. She wrapped a broad belt around my left thigh and calf, forming a triangle. Then she externally rotated my hip to stretch contracted tendons—until I winced.

"Can you take it any longer?"

"Yes, don't stop now," said I, hoping that, magically, I would be able to get up and run as I used to run. "Do your worst."

She then had me walk up and down two flights of stairs, using the handrails. Then she got me ready to run, taking out her stopwatch.

She asked, "Where did you like to run before you came here? Or were you mainly a cyclist?"

I launched into an answer, this time deliberately testing my ability to use words parsimoniously.

"I like running in Discovery Park, or Volunteer Park, or on the Burke-Gilman Trail. But my favorite run in Seattle is in Myrtle Edwards Park, along the Sound. You can see Mount Rainier and the cranes in the port, which look like enormous giraffes. And there you will find my favorite outdoor sculpture, *Adjacent, Against, Upon.* You can almost see a giant slab of granite crawling like a huge, determined lizard, starting flat on its belly and inching up onto a platform, getting there at last and mounting its perch. I forget the name of the sculptor. I think it's a woman."

"Well said," said AND. "You'll get there too. I live near Myrtle Edwards Park, and I run there all the time, but I've never noticed that sculpture."

"Maybe one day, I'll run with you and show you."

"Maybe. But for now, let's see *this* lizard run."

The lizard ran.

Soon, Denise picked me up in front of the hospital.

"How did it go?"

"I ran a hundred yards."

"What a man," said Denise. "I brought you a sandwich."

CHAPTER TWENTY-SIX

Observing in Dr. Bell's Clinic

The play's the thing
Wherein I'll catch the conscience of the king.

– William Shakespeare, *Hamlet*, act 2, scene 2

THE NEXT TIME I SAW CHRIS AND JIMMY WAS IN DR. BELL'S CLINIC, where I was spending one afternoon a week for ten weeks, observing along with whichever resident who was on duty that day in order to help determine whether I had sufficiently recrafted myself to be a doctor. I was pleased to encounter Dr. Shenouda, who would soon be moving on to the National Institute of Health in Washington, D.C. He had occasionally stopped by my room when I was a patient down the hall. I thanked him again for working with my daughter Margaret to prevent me from moldering in a skilled nursing facility. He was gracious, as always, and he thanked me for having pointed out a seminal paper in his field, from the 1950s, that showed that patients with supposedly mild head injuries often had findings of significant neuronal loss at autopsy—if their families permitted this study, so gruesome to the layman.

"The brain is sometimes more delicate than even we suspect," I had said to Dr. Shenouda, not wanting to listen to myself.

Jimmy was the first of the brain-injured patients I saw that day. He had made gains in coordination, actually now walking with a walker. He was also more cognitively apt, but far from his former promising self. His mother's disappointment was more evident than her pleasure in his progress.

A week later, in Dr. Bell's clinic, I saw a forty-two-year-old Hispanic male who just happened to share my Hispanic name. "Victor Manuel," he said. He was beaten badly in 2009 while working as a security officer, having already suffered head injuries ten years earlier, along with an old bullet wound in his right foot, which was still painful, impairing his gait. Since his recent beating, he suffered from a right-facial droop and drooling, as well as post-traumatic stress disorder, speech difficulties, mood swings, forgetfulness, head pain at the crown ("not a headache"), and insomnia. Occasionally, he fell down. With Ambien, he was able to get "good sleep of five hours." On the day I saw him, he reported nine pounds of weight loss over the last three weeks.

Being a compassionate physician is not the same as being a

physician who actually identifies with his patient. But there I was, worried that I, too, would be hobbling into the brain injury clinic in three years, drooling and suffering cognitive problems—a former security officer of medicine, no longer robust, but glad to be alive and able to have five good hours of sleep every night.

That day I also saw a fifty-year-old man who had undergone surgery for a large left-sided meningioma, a benign tumor inside the head but outside the brain. The mass of the neoplasm had compressed the parietal lobe of his dominant hemisphere, leaving him with right-sided weakness and sensory disturbance, as well as some cognitive deficits. He was now making a good recovery, his brain having been merely compressed, not necessarily permanently injured. I celebrated his progressive return to his usual self with a newfound empathy.

After the resident and I had completed our examinations of this improving patient, Dr. Bell came in. She was naturally interested in the patient's ability to feel objects with his right hand, for that information registers in the left parietal lobe, which had been compressed. With his eyes closed, she put a quarter into his outstretched hand and asked him to identify the object. She was satisfied when he said, "A coin."

I said, "Let me show you something."

I asked the patient to close his eyes again and extend his right hand, palm up. I put a dime on his palm and asked him to identify it precisely.

"You mean what type of coin it is?" he asked.

"Yes."

"This is a dime."

"How do you know?

"From its size and its serrated edge. It's not a penny."

"Keeping your eyes closed, tell me which side is up, heads or tails."

He rubbed the coin with his thumb and forefinger and said, "This is heads."

Feeling his oats, the brain-injured neurologist said to the estimable Dr. Bell, "You see, with this simple test one can check both the peripheral sensory nerves in the hand and the central processing of sensation in the contralateral parietal lobe. The patient's peripheral nerves in the right hand can or cannot appreciate a serrated edge and distinguish the different smoothness between heads and tails. And his left parietal lobe can or cannot draw on previous experience with American coinage to interpret the incoming data."

"Thank you," said the sincere, supportive Dr. Bell. "That's going to be my favorite part of the neurologic examination."

Her tone meant everything to me. I said thank you to her but neglected to mention how much she'd helped me in transforming myself from patient to doctor.

Yet another patient from that day, also about fifty years old, had suffered a rupture of an arterio-venous malformation of the brain, which caused severe bleeding and led to a technically successful operation. Nevertheless, she remained exhausted, calling in sick repeatedly, now more than a year after her surgery. She couldn't make herself get out of bed. She slept through her alarm. Though she had been commended for her work before her bleed, her supervisor was threatening to dismiss her.

Dr. Bell was kind but firm with this failing woman, prescribing more aerobics, more stimulants, and more antidepressants. I could not tell if she was communicating a doubt about the woman's capacity or if I was projecting my own worries onto this poor woman. I fought that fatigue daily, even eight months after my head injury. Though present on Thursdays only, with no responsibility, I wanted to help this administrator to remake herself. But that was for another day.

Meanwhile, I would do more aerobic exercise myself, for there is evidence that aerobic exercise improves cognition in traumatic brain injury, even in Parkinson's disease and Alzheimer's disease.

My last patient in Dr. Bell's clinic was an eighteen-year-old young man who had also suffered a ruptured cerebral vascular malformation. A tangle of poorly formed arteries suddenly exploded, his fate complicated by a stroke related to his surgery to repair the vascular mess. He now presented with profound depression, seizures, a right visual field cut, and aphasia, all because of the damage to his dominant (left) hemisphere. He soldiered on.

And I soldiered on. Dr. Bell smiled as I left. When Denise picked me up in front of the hospital, I was again worn out and glad to put down my cane.

CHAPTER TWENTY-SEVEN

Work Works

You shall this twelvemonth term, from day to day,
Visit the speechless sick, and still converse
With groaning wretches; and your task shall be,
With all the fierce endeavor of your wit
To enforce the pained impotent to smile.
– William Shakespeare, *Love's Labor's Lost*, act 5, scene 2

After participating in Dr. Bell's brain injury clinic, I was permitted to drive, with the recommendation that someone ride shotgun with me. As I drove with Denise, I provided her with a running commentary on my thoughts. I would say,

"I'm assuming that fourteen Chinese orphans are waiting to cross at the intersection just ahead, and they are unpredictable. One of them might run out in front of me."

I went back to work at the end of February, working for only two hours that day. I was diminished but hopeful, buoyed up by my new antidepressant. Feeling this way reminded me of being initiated into the life of a medical intern, into that intense year of sleep deprivation and wit sharpening, and immersion in sorrow. As an intern, I felt a near sacred sense of usefulness, a strange calm amid hectic days and nights. Exhausted most of the time, I was nevertheless grateful for the capacity to treat asthma attacks, heart attacks, pneumonias, and AIDS-related fevers in the middle of the night. After a lifetime of feeling semi crippled, half deaf, and visually impaired (not only from myopia, but from the lack of binocular vision), I was made whole at the age of forty-five, when I finished my residency in neurology, in the fictive way anybody can imagine himself whole. Knocked down in Kenya and now climbing back up at sixty-seven, I recalled what it felt like to be confident. But recall is only a tantalizing hint of a possible future.

By chance, there was a staff meeting at the Seattle Golf Club just after I'd started working again. I put on the suit and bow tie that I wore to walk Margaret down the aisle at her wedding eighteen months earlier. Worried about making a fool of myself, I was nevertheless pleased to be there, alive and with a commanding view of Puget Sound over the trees.

Bill Schneider, the CEO, rose to welcome us, as he had done so many times before. He is a tough customer, a powerful man who worked his way through college by driving big trucks, a former union negotiator. Many found him overbearing, but he built the best community hospital I have ever seen, with the finest nurses and a top medical staff. He helped me build the first service for the care of acute stroke in Seattle.

At the podium, he said, "I usually start this meeting by telling you about what we have done in the past year to take better care of our patients and what we are going to do in the future. But this evening I want to start by focusing on one of our own. Dr. Erlich is here after going through hell in Kenya. I think we ought to welcome him."

I got a standing ovation, immensely gratifying, and frightening too, because I could tell from the applause that most of those present thought I would never make it back. And I knew that this was true of my own thinking for a long time. In fact, I wasn't feeling so well at the moment.

The first chance I had, I stopped by the administrative wing of the hospital to thank Mr. Schneider for his kindness. I ran into him immediately.

"I heard you worked hard to get me back to Seattle. I want to thank you," I told him.

For a tough guy, he knew how to smile.

"I would do it again in a minute. Say, what did they do for you over there at the university hospital?"

"They asked me to define the word *apple*. This is true. I said it was a monocot, domesticated by the Chinese, who invented grafting, which is the only way to propagate the plant since the tree cannot propagate itself, not even by Johnny Appleseed. I also said *apple* was sometimes used metaphorically, as in the phrase 'the apple of my eye'—which, by the way, is a mistranslation of the Hebrew phrase,

Ishun ha-ayin, which means 'the pupil of the eye.' I think I got into trouble for that. They kept telling me I was repetitive. They deduct points if you say too much."

"They are correct. The definition of *apple* is simple: Apple is the best corporation in the world. What else did they ask you?"

"They asked me to define the word *glove*. This is true. I couldn't figure out why they were asking such simple questions. Maybe there was some psychological aspect of the question that I missed, like how I would handle myself when I was being annoyed. But I think they had already learned that my patience, for which I had earned a kind of praise, had its limits. I tried to keep it simple by saying that a glove was a covering for the hand, a protection against the cold, or a glove could be used to play a sport, like baseball or boxing, or to perform surgery. Then I shot off my mouth, probably getting myself into trouble again, saying that 'hand in glove,' is a metaphor, said of people in cahoots."

"When did you lose your patience?"

"Often, but I knew enough to bite my tongue. Once, though, when I was just starting to walk and go to the bathroom by myself, I came back to my room to use the bathroom. Without bothering to inform me, they moved a woman into the adjoining room, which shared a bathroom with my room. My new neighbor needed absolute privacy because she was on chemotherapy and her urine was contaminated. I found the bathroom locked and a commode in the middle of my room. I had many guests. The nurses knew that it would not work well for me to have a can in the middle of my room; that's what my father called a toilet, 'the can.' I was fuming. I got the nursing supervisor and told her I wanted to leave. Luckily, Vicky, was standing right there, and she calmed me down."

"How did you resolve the problem?"

"They apologized and found me a different room with a private bathroom."

"Welcome home," said Mr. Schneider. "You sound like your old self, too wordy, as you said. Be hand in glove with us. We'll deal with the plumbing."

CHAPTER TWENTY-EIGHT

Ritalin for Forlorn Fatigue

For of the soul the body form doth take:
For soul is form, and doth the body make.
– Edmund Spenser, "An Hymn in Honour of Love"

RETURNING TO WORK WAS NOT STRAIGHTFORWARD. I SIMPLY DID NOT have my old stamina. For weeks I couldn't take emergency call at night or on weekends. Because of fatigue, I had to be in bed by eight in the evening, sometimes getting through no more than one page of reading before losing attention.

One day of rehab, a substitute who was making rounds for Dr.

Song, said, “It takes at least a year for brain-injured patients to go back to work.”

Her words echoed in my head. The Saturday before my discharge, I was visited by yet another stand-in attending. He asked me if anything was bothering me.

I said that I was peculiarly sleepy all day, having done nothing at all strenuous.

The doctor quickly replied, “Fatigue is typical for brain-injured patients. It can be quite severe and go on for a long time.”

“If I’m sleepy because I’m brain injured, why wasn’t I sleepy last week?”

“Brain injury is funny that way.”

I didn’t find it funny. Here I was, back at work but with no stamina. I began my return to practice by seeing in follow-up a few former patients whom I knew well, building up so slowly that I feared I would never wake up.

The more energy I put into arousing myself, the more fatigued I felt. My friend Dr. David Warth came to visit me at home one evening, careful not to bother me too late. Sheepishly, he told me that my friends were worried. They thought I was pushing myself too hard. I was digging myself deeper and deeper into fatigue, making myself my own enemy as I fought on.

The next day, after a mere two hours of work, I returned to the UW for an appointment with Dr. Kurt Johnson. He beamed his usual confidence in me, but he told me about a brain-injured physician whom he had recently coached back to work. The man published a successful paper in a reputable journal and had no trouble handling the cases that came before him, but he couldn’t keep up with his workload, especially the electronic medical records. This crushed his confidence.

I returned home to make myself read a few journal articles while I ate the chicken Denise had prepared for me.

Shortly thereafter, I had a meeting with Dr. Bell, as a patient myself in the very clinic in which I had postured as an all-knowing neurologist. I filled out the usual intake forms, reporting that I had virtually no pain and no falls or mishaps of any kind. The medical assistant then walked me to Dr. Bell's consulting room. I explained to the good doctor that I was more fatigued now than I'd ever been in the hospital.

Dr. Bell, like others before her, told me that my experience was typical of patients with a brain injury.

"Everything is organized for you in the hospital, even if you don't need it. Every patient finds it difficult to go home."

I remembered how hard I'd fought to stay hospitalized, somehow intuiting that I wouldn't improve as fast at home as I had in the hospital. I did not want to go home then, and now I didn't like who I was at home, or at work. I knew that brain-injured patients sometimes respond well to Ritalin, the medication given to hyperactive children. That's what I wanted. But I worried that this type of stimulation in adults could produce heart disease, the problem that killed my Zadie.

"Yes, we used to worry about the coronary complications of Ritalin," said Dr. Bell, taking just the right tone with me. "But a large recent study shows that there is no significant long-term cardiac risk with a judicious use of drugs of this type."

That sentence alone enabled me to put out of my mind the fact that my zadie suffered his first heart attack when he was sixty-one. He, after all, had been a smoker.

"Start with five milligrams twice a day," continued Dr. Bell, again exuding care and confidence. "You can go up to ten milligrams four times a day. I'll leave it up to you."

I used Ritalin for five months, never taking more than ten milligrams twice a day. The drug worked miraculously, persuading my healing brain that it didn't need so much sleep after all. In its normal state, the brain needs sleep so that it can repair itself after wearing itself down, firing away the whole day long. The healing brain requires even more sleep, having so much more to repair.

Soon I was working full days, then taking emergency calls on an occasional weeknight, then on call for full weekends. I was almost my old self, but this wasn't the same as being fully energetic. To compensate, I worked seven days a week in my office to face stacks of charts on my desk and dictate notes about previous appointments.

I wanted desperately to be one of those who came home from World War II to buy a tract home in Venice, California. I was not going to be a semi-crazed, discharged soldier who came home to the bean field at the dead end of Commonwealth Avenue, content to sleep in high weeds woven into safe caves over warm soil, liberated from European cold and South Pacific heat.

And then I learned that Bill Schneider was retiring as CEO of Northwest Hospital, and his replacement was a nurse administrator from Harborview Hospital. She must have heard from her connections there about the state I was in when I was there, for she decided, without speaking to me, that I should no longer be director of the stroke program.

CHAPTER

TWENTY-NINE

Determination to See

I sometimes hold it half a sin
To put in words the grief I feel:
For words, like Nature, half reveal
And half conceal the Soul within.

But, for the unquiet heart and brain,
A use in measured language lies;
The sad mechanic exercise,
Like dull narcotics, numbing pain.

– Alfred Lord Tennyson,
"In Memoriam A. H. H.," section 5

One evening, after soldiering through a day in the office, I got a call from my daughter Shala, the psychiatrist, telephoning from Vermont. I told her I was working, not yet taking calls from the emergency room, but working almost full time otherwise. I explained that I was not really my old self, but I was putting in weekend time to dictate charts so I could appear efficient.

"Work works," I said, repeating the advice with which I had sent her to Yale, and then to medical school.

She was pleased by my progress.

"You're the most determined person I know," she said.

I knew instantly that she was thinking about a stubbornness that she had often claimed to be in my character. And I knew that she was thinking of one event in particular that took place at Lower Mill Pond on Cape Cod in August of 1981, just before I started medical school. She was ten years old, so frightened to dive off our dock that we had to try another approach. She would stand on my shoulders as I stood in water up to my ribs. I held her hands as she dove from there.

On one occasion, she kicked my eyeglasses into the water. I quickly triangulated where we were, using landmarks on shore. Then, with Shala safely ashore, I walked about, feeling the pond floor with my feet, staying within what I had calculated to be the relevant circle. After an hour or so, I gave up, only to resume the task daily for a week, until I finally stepped on my glasses and recovered them, lifting them up with my foot, like a monkey. We went back to New York the next day. Shala remembered the story.

"Is that what makes me the most determined person you know?" I asked her.

"Yes, and other things too."

"Like what?"

"You were a published and tenured professor of literature with three children and a mortgage. You were determined to go to medical school, and you did it—quite successfully, I might add. And in medical school, you taught English lit at night, determined not to go into debt. People thought you were brave to give up tenure, but I knew you were more determined than brave."

"Do you remember that I was determined to send you to college knowing Shakespeare? I think I took you to fifty productions of Shakespeare before you went to Yale. You had already met Peaseblossom in the ladies' room when we saw *A Midsummer Night's Dream* on the roof of Riverside Church."

"I remember that."

"What else do you remember?"

"I remember Benedick talking himself into the idea that it was OK that he loved Beatrice. 'The world must be peopled.'"

Oh, I thought, *how good it would be if I could, like Benedick, come to terms so easily with my needs!* But I feared my mind had the provenance not of Benedick, but of Dogberry, the Shakespearean policeman in *Much Ado About Nothing*, the unlikely brake on the runaway sadism of Don John, whose unprovoked hatred cannot be stopped by his intelligent brother or anybody else. It falls to goofy Dogberry, who, in his bumbling way, stumbles onto the plot that was missed by wiser souls. It is Dogberry who proclaims the innocence of the maliciously slandered Hero. It is Dogberry who accidentally champions executive function, just when the nominal executives fail.

Shakespeare's point is that an unlikely and unreliable reversal has occurred, with Dogberry governing the governor. For private love and public order to prevail, this reversal must be reversed. A well-groomed executive function must trump Dogberry's idiocy, which was only accidentally effective.

Oh, may my own accidents give me the power of Dogberry, but without his dogged stupidity. May I remember to reverse the reversed brakes the next time I take a British cycling tour.

CHAPTER

THIRTY

A New Ride

The grand symphonic piece that is consciousness encompasses . . . the wider-than-the-sky imagery created in the cooperation of cerebral cortex and subcortical structures, all harmoniously stitched together, in ceaseless forward motion, interrupted only by sleep, anesthesia, brain dysfunction, or death . . . a collective voice set free in a song of affirmation.

– Antonio Damasio,
Self Comes to Mind: Constructing the Conscious Brain

Moss and Peg came to my house to take me on my first bike ride in fifteen months. I had cycled with them on arduous climbs in the French Alps and the Pyrenees. They would mock me for the tools and equipment I carried in a fanny pack, up four thousand feet of elevation from Briançon to the Col d'Izoard. Moss would lift up my pack at the café near the summit, and say, "This weighs more than my bike."

I would reply, "That's why I'm the last one up here."

Moss is a highly intelligent non-practicing attorney, big-hearted with a wry sense of humor, an expert cyclist. Before my discharge from UW Rehab, he came to my room, smiling.

"Peg and I have talked this over. When you leave here, you're going to need some help. You can come live with us. I am not working, and Mariah is at college. I can work around your schedule. If you need something in the middle of the night, I'll be there. I'll drive you to your outpatient appointments. It won't be a bother."

I was too frightened of dependency to accept his generous offer, though I wound up being even more dependent on Denise and my sister, Nan. The difference was that I was at least paying the rent. Moss's magnanimity was extraordinary, matched only by a few other friends: David Warth, Debbie Scharnikow, Marie-Louise Mercer, and Jourdan Gottlieb. And there was David Brumer, who looked after me until he died suddenly of cardiac arrest on a hike in the Cascades, leaving a wife and two sons bereft, just as I was going back to work. As my mother often said, "We don't know what to worry about."

And I was blessed to share the weave of my recovery with Dr. Joseph McCreery, who applied his deep therapeutic skills to securing that recovery. Yes, he continued my antidepressant, but his mastery of the art of medicine (he began his career by working as a medic while a teenager, served as a family doctor, then undertook a second residency to become a psychiatrist) is what helped me emerge in the dawn's light.

On my maiden voyage on a bike after my accident, Moss's job was to ride in front of me and keep me from going too fast or too far. Peg is a first-rate cardiologist. Her job was to follow me closely, and, I quipped, "pronounce me dead, if necessary." Those were the rules.

In the past, I did not take short bike rides, preferring something in the range of fifty to a hundred miles. This time, we would go ten miles.

Moss held my bike while I tried to straddle it. I was embarrassed by my inability to throw my right leg over the bike's seat. Damn it, my physical therapists had told me to stretch, but I'd failed them. Moss had to stretch my leg up and over the seat, which was surprisingly high.

Moss said, "You can speak French, so you can straddle. How do you say 'straddle' in French?"

"*Enfourcher*, from *fourche*, a pitchfork. Same word as *fourchette*, you know, the way you reach across the table with your *fourchette* in France, spearing anything that your fellow cyclists fail to eat."

Peg, taking pictures, said, "If Moss is at the table, nothing goes back to the kitchen."

"Touché," said the indefatigable Moss. "Well then, now that you've straddled the bike, let us fork away."

I survived the ten miles. Peg took a picture of Moss and me with our bikes. I am the man in the orange jersey, paunchy from lack of exercise.

CHAPTER

THIRTY-ONE

The Monster Reconfigured

Behavior is rooted in integration. The patterned nature of the activities of the roof-brain [i.e., the cerebral cortex] expresses integration by its patterning . . . Dissolving pattern after dissolving pattern will, the long day through, without remission melt into and succeed each other."

– Sir Charles Scott Sherrington, *Man on His Nature*, 1940

I BEGAN TO TRAVEL AGAIN, TO VERMONT TO SEE SHALA; TO ATLANTA WITH Aaron to see Margaret; to New York to attend a conference in memory of Dr. Fred Plum, my esteemed professor of neurology; then again to New York, where I stayed with old friends from the time I was a training neurologist at New York Hospital. Nahma Sandrow, the doyenne of Yiddish studies, and her husband, William Meyers, one of America's best photographers, helped me reconnect myself to them and to a world I had thought lost.

Billy kindly interrupted his writing and said, "Let's have fun," so we visited the Metropolitan Museum of Art. I was surprised to stumble onto an exhibit of work by the eighteenth-century German artist and entertainer, Matthias Buchinger. While living in Amsterdam in 1705, he commissioned an etching of himself in his typical guise as a dwarf with bony knobs for hands. He stands (probably kneels) on a cushion, disguising his trickery under an ample coat. Despite his supposedly gross deformities (that's not a human bone under his left sleeve), he excelled in drawing and even signed in red ink his reportedly commissioned portrait. And he made sure that this portrait included, on the desk next to him, all the tools he used expertly, including a drawing of a flower, a quill and ink pot, a pair of dice, a German hackbrett (a musical instrument resembling a dulcimer), and a rifle.

Buchinger earned money and fame from his monstrosity, actually a fiction of phony disability and narcissistic self-display. He composed his brain's mixed drives to shoot, gamble, draw, and play music, all the while attracting women (at the time of his portrait, he was married to his fourth wife). Though Buchinger produced naught but a freak show, he enacted a deep truth. To a large degree, we create ourselves. Our artfulness triumphs over monstrosity.

My accidents are etched into my memory. I am unable to follow Oberon's advice near the end of *A Midsummer Night's Dream*, "Think no more of this night's accidents / But as the fierce vexation of a dream." Rather than vexation, my accidents led to a creative healing and a forgiveness of hard fortune.

Much is made of the pervasive theme of forgiveness in Shakespeare's last plays. Evil is overcome and sin, forgiven in *Pericles, Prince of Tyre; The Winter's Tale; Cymbeline;* and *The Tempest.* Shakespeare's vision of forgiveness arises from his understanding that sin is not so much a religious deviation, but the inevitable outcome of an unstrung mind bereft of art. Iago in *Othello,* Angelo in *Measure for Measure,* Claudius in *Hamlet,* Don John in *Much Ado About Nothing,* Lady Macbeth, and Richard III, are all diabolic, but the disharmonized mind, not the devil, makes this so. And this difference is all-important; we can do nothing about the imaginary devil, but a troubled mind can be reharmonized.

The mind possesses a self-healing creativity, as I learned from hard experience. As a recovered patient, I was reminded again of Dr. Sacks' conclusion to *A Leg to Stand On:* "A perfect communion lay upon the land. This peacefulness had a quality of thanksgiving and praise, a kind of silent, holy intensity; but a silence which was also thanksgiving and song . . . I felt that all the world itself was one vast hymn."

Dr. Sacks' epiphany arises from the fundamental drive of the human brain to find harmonious meaning. This drive, itself based on a composition of neural networks, underlies health, well-being, and recovery from injury. Composition and the making of hymns are exclusively human, unless you count the weaving of a bird's nest and the consequent bird song. Our kind of composition is more complex, not merely utilitarian, but also aesthetic, as in this painting from France's Chauvet Cave:

Tattooed on the cave wall with a dark pigment some thirty-two thousand years ago, the image shows a chieftain, enlarged, who leads his four shorter warriors to battle or to hunt, with the lines of arrows, bows, and legs all composed. The curve of the marching men mirrors that of the deadly bows.

This old composition is a harbinger of a design on an ancient Greek vase, crafted ages later, in about 530 BC, when the medium and the message hadn't much changed. According to the Metropolitan Museum of Art, the vase was likely the trophy for the victor of a race.

But it is much more. It integrates the urge to compete with the need to live beautifully. The twenty limbs are interwoven, and the spaces between them are balanced and composed.

The artist in the cave may have had in mind a memorial to departed hunters or warriors, a significantly different theme from the Greek trophy, but the Ice Age composition is of the same kind as that on the Greek vase. The cave painting and the vase are first and foremost human creations, crafted weaves of aggression and beauty, of leadership and obeisance, of life and death. Also captured is the cave artist's urge to bring forth harmony to overcome its opposite, death and dissolution, which is, after all, the purpose of war and hunting. This aesthetic expression in the cave is similar to the vase artist's drive to lift male rivalry above the merely physical, to the sublime. The cave and the vase are one, expressions of the brain's urge to live victoriously, joyfully, and harmoniously. We live to create, and we create to live.

What neuronal mechanism allows the brain to integrate thoughts and feelings and then transfer an aesthetic facsimile of its thinking to a vase or a cave, to a canvas or to a mode of living? The founder of modern neurophysiology, Sir Charles Scott Sherrington, described the qualities of just such a harmonizing mechanism, though he did not know the necessary physical details. The belief that there is a kind of integration or harmony to thought, says Sherrington, "dominated medicine and biology through Alexandrian, Christian, Arabian, and Jewish learning."

For two thousand five hundred years, the attempt to base a theory of thought on an examination of the brain's physical properties failed. When inspected, the raw, dissected brain did not look like it could do much thinking or feeling on its own. Thus, from the time of Aristotle's *De Anima* on, philosophers and scientists assumed that there must be a non-material animating force that allowed the brain to generate well-composed thought and feeling. The non-material soul must animate the blob of the brain. Or, the alignment of the stars must make us think and act, as was case of the "star-crossed lovers" Romeo and Juliet. Or was it the muses, or the angels, or the devil who moved us? Descartes tried to find the animating force that allowed mind to arise from the material brain, but he failed, thus perpetuating the mind-brain conundrum, still unsolved.

Even the discovery in the nineteenth century that the brain's living power arose from its electrical activity did not solve the problem. "The best technique for studying the activity of the brain and nerve is today electrical," says Sherrington, but not even the electrical hum of the brain could be shown to yield mind. And there Sherrington left the problem. Breathing was explained by revealing the working of the lungs; the circulation of blood, by the mechanics of the heart; and ambulation, by nerves moving muscles. The human body could be seen as a special kind of machine, "all of it," says Sherrington, "except one factor. There science stopped and stared at an unexpected residue which remained."

That unexpected residue is the self-harmonizing mind. We know how the heart pumps out blood, but how does the brain pump out a conscious, well-woven thought? Sherrington didn't know, but long before him, Plato came close to a good answer. This giant of philosophy and composition believed that the human brain endowed itself with aesthetic capacity, or "soul." Perhaps the gods or the muses assisted, but it is human music that helps train the soul. In *The Republic,* Plato says the following:

> Musical training is a more potent instrument than any other, because rhythm and harmony find their way into the secret places of the soul, on which they mightily fasten, imparting grace, and making the soul of him who is rightly educated. . . . He who has received this true education of the inner being will most shrewdly perceive omissions or fault in art and nature, and . . . receives into his soul the good.

With this kind of rehabilitated capacity, but without the ability to sing, I remade my life. I fell into harmony the harp-playing King David, after whom my father was named, with Plato and Galen, with Sir Francis Bacon, with Sherrington and Shakespeare, hoping to illustrate how mindful music mended a medical man. The brain, itself a work of art, is an organ fit to shape the art medicine.

And thus, students of the art of medicine benefit from the study of art itself, such as Nikolai Mikhailovich Plyusnin's 1873 portrayal of David, the future King who uses his harp to minister to the current, despondent, and soul-blasted King Saul. The Russian painter conceives the scene so that the ancient Hebrew, now a youthful poet and musician, plays to his patient, who casts his head downward, himself unable to muster the creativity of the psalmist.

David's harp still plays in my mind. As long as this harp remains unbroken, my devotion to artful medicine will thrive.

CODA

The Neurology of Harmony

Imagine, for example, a group of musicians, let us say a string quartet. As each member of the quartet plays his individual instrument, he both sends to and receives from his fellow musicians "signals" about the sound, volume, rhythm, accent, and tone quality of the music. Each player is carrying on an individual dialogue with the other players, together creating a sound at any given moment. There is no conductor. . . . Just as the shape and overall sound of the quartet's performance is created by the various sounds from moment to moment, so, too, categorizations emerge from the brain's relating one coherent response to another and another.

– Israel Rosenfield, *The Strange, Familiar, and Forgotten: An Anatomy of Consciousness*, 1995

By chance, it so happened that as I was falling off my bike in Kenya, a paper I wrote came to press in the *Einstein Journal of Biology and Medicine,* timed to coincide with the silver anniversary of my graduation from the Albert Einstein College of Medicine. Without my being aware of any specific relevance to my own brain's way of thinking, this theoretical work allowed me to conceptualize how I used art to live, feel, and heal. In "Cognition Without a Neural Code: How a Folded Cortex Might Think by Harmonizing Its Own Electromagnetic Fields," I offered an explanation, based on current neuroscience, of how the one hundred–billion neurons in the brain might craft a thought rapidly and accurately. I found, unexpectedly, that the novel mechanism I was describing also provided a neurologic explanation for the human creation of art.

My recovery from the accidents of my life, large and small, has led me to the conviction that a meaningful life must include a capacity to bring harmony and beauty to what Hamlet calls "the slings and arrows of outrageous fortune." Yes, I have grit and determination. Yes, I had the support of loving children and the best of friends. And yes, I underwent rehabilitation at one of the country's best centers for brain injury. But there was something more to my recovery. If marshaling my version of the human aesthetic capacity had the healing powers I claim, then there must be a neurologic mechanism that makes these powers effective. Rosenfield, quoted in this chapter's epigraph, intimates that there must be a material mechanism in the brain that composes a harmonized thought in the way a string quartet produces well-tempered music without a conductor: "As each member of the quartet plays his individual instrument, he both sends to and receives from his fellow musicians 'signals' about the sound, volume, rhythm, accent, and tone quality of the music." If the brain is like a self-harmonizing string quartet, precisely how might the brain send signals to itself and integrate them?

Let me summarize my answer to this question, which was published synchronously with my crash in Kenya. Though my hypothesis about the brain's mechanism for thinking and healing is naught but a theory, bereft of the necessary experimental support, it offers a material model of mind that could actually arise from brain, both in a normal state and in an injured state.

In neuroscience, we often speak of how clusters of neurons in one area send "messages" along axonal "wires" to other clusters in other areas. Since each neuron makes up to ten thousand connections with other neurons, a multitude of messages are presumably zinging about all the time. Through "axonal messaging," clusters of cells can modify the firing of other clusters through synaptic modulation (synapses are those exact spots where an axon touches and thus "communicates" with another neuron). After much to-and-fro palaver, with axonal traffic leading to multiple synaptic modulations, which in turn leads to more traffic and more modulation, great pools of brain activity reach a consensus that constitutes a "thought" or a "feeling." Brain injury jars precisely this ability to come to a sensible consensus.

This traditional theory of how the normal brain thinks has many problems, most of which are ignored. How axons can carry messages, and in what code, remains a mystery. How the brain rapidly coordinates its various centers is a related mystery. No neural code by which "messages" might be sent has ever been found. Further, the total time required by all this hypothetical axonal messaging and synaptic modulation, given the known speed of these activities, far exceeds the time it takes humans to think and act. The old saw in neuroscience that "neurons that fire together wire together" is simply too vague to offer a useful explanation for the complex process of integrating all the aspects of a complex thought. How do hundreds of millions of neurons firing together wire together quickly enough to produce a novel thought? How do they avoid cacophony? How do they become coherent, focused, and relevant? How do all those firing neurons that represent extraneous matter get silenced? Since every new thought is distinct from prior thoughts, how does the firing and wiring change fast enough to keep up with the speed of human thinking?

What process orchestrates the music of thought? What effects of firing neurons could lead to the equivalent of Rosenfield's hypothetical beautifully performing string quartet, in which "each player is carrying on an individual dialogue with the other players"? If we knew the answers to these questions, we might be able to learn how the brain restores itself when it is out of tune.

If the rapid speed of thought cannot adequately be explained simply by stating that what fires together wires together, what other explanation might be offered? Let us assume that previous learning and experience do fix patterns of connectivity, with synaptic modulation serving as the record of long-term learning, but not the mechanism of thinking on the fly. Let us also assume what is well known, that long axons can activate distant centers of the brain simply by firing without a specific code, as in simple reflexes, say when one spits out tea that is too hot. But if we don't have a reliable code being sent down axons, and synaptic change is too slow, how does active thinking proceed? If we can document that the brain has another way of integrating the many parts of a thought, perhaps we can construct a coherent model of thought.

And, indeed, there is a known but ignored way that the brain can integrate its multitudinous firings. All that axonal connectivity produces coherent patterns of electromagnetic fields, whether or not there is any messaging along axons. While studying patients with seizures and other cerebral dysfunctions, clinicians record these fields using electroencephalograms and magneto-encephalograms, the former focusing on electric fields, and the latter, on magnetic fields emanating from the firing brain. The study of these fields, their rhythms, and their patterns of coherence, has led to a vast medical literature. Specific electromagnetic fields can be correlated with various stages of sleep; with various kinds of seizures; with various forms of toxicity, such as alcohol. More to my purpose, specific patterns of recorded fields can be correlated with specific kinds of thinking. Lists of nouns spoken to a subject undergoing a magnetoencephalogram produce a distinct pattern, while a list of adjectives read to the same subject produces other recognizable electromagnetic fields. Distinct odors produce still other specific patterns in the brain's organization of its electromagnetic fields. Different patterns of axonal firing lead to different patterns of recorded fields, and these fields seem to be part of the physical basis of thought.

I discovered that I was not the only one to suggest that the brain's electromagnetic fields might play a role in thought. Norman Doidge, in *The Brain's Way of Healing*, summarizes some previous work by other scientists. "[Karl] Lashley appears to have been the first neuroscientist to propose . . . that learning and skills are encoded not 'in' specific neurons, or even 'in' the connections between neurons, but 'in' the *cumulative wave patterns* that are the result of all the neurons firing together."

The fields by themselves are not thoughts. Rather, according to my hypothesis, they help the brain organize itself into a pattern of firing that constitutes a specific thought, which is also integrated with a specific pattern of feeling. Coherent, meaningful thoughts and feelings become, if they are sufficiently vivid, conscious and memorable, thus contributing to self-consciousness.

Electromagnetic fields have been biologically active since the beginning of biologic time. Some primitive bacteria use magnetosomes to align themselves with Earth's magnetic field so that they can navigate through water to a source of nutrition. Sharks navigate and hunt by using their ampullae of Lorenzini, which work as microscopic radar stations strung along their flanks, allowing these hunters to pick up electromagnetic signals emanating from prey or from target destinations miles away. They can swim thousands of miles across open oceans without getting lost. Blind mole rats tunnel for long distances underground, able to navigate successfully without vision by using their sensitivity to Earth's magnetic fields.

The human brain, much later evolved and with a finer capacity than the brains of sharks and mole rats, would be capable of adapting its self-generated electromagnetic fields to craft a visual image in Technicolor out of the fragmented electrical signals coming from the retina. And then, by broadcasting further fields from that integrated visual image, the firing brain might fuse that image with meaning and history. That well-woven tapestry can then be applied to an appropriate response. The human brain acts as described by Theseus at the end of *A Midsummer Night's Dream*:

> And as imagination bodies forth
> The forms of things unknown, the poet's pen
> Turns them to shapes, and gives to airy nothing
> A local habitation and a name.

In order for the brain to convert airy nothings into specific, coherent patterns of thought, there has to be an instrument capable of doing so. The mind's evolved capacity to seek one harmonious state after another is, I believe, the fountainhead of the human drive to create art, including the healing arts.

What might be the physical mechanism of that harmonization? To compose a painting, a painter uses brushstrokes. What does the brain do to compose a thought? In my published paper, I try to demonstrate how each pattern of neuronal connectivity automatically generates a specific electromagnetic field, each with its own identity, its own signature, the result of its individual twists and turns as it follows its unique pathway. Each unique field, like those of individual radio stations, stimulates only those circuits in the brain tuned to that signature. Just as a phone call into a large crowd rings only in the pocket of the one person carrying the right cell, so too will the specific fields generated by every firing circuit in the brain stimulate other circuits with receptors tuned to it.

That which is stimulated fires, generating a new field of its own, and that field both stimulates higher-order circuits and stabilizes the lower-order circuits that are broadcasting to it. A thought, I proposed, arises from the broadcast of biologically active electromagnetic fields which self-integrate as they come to rest momentarily after broadcasting and return-broadcasting to each other, with all circuits that are still active forming a complex thought or feeling. All neuronal circuits that do not fit in, that do not harmonize, die down, thus spontaneously eliminating the noise of extraneous matter, leaving the surviving harmony to ring out as clear as a bell. The fleeting harmony that thus emerges is the passing thought, lasting until the brain moves on. "To use an analogy," adds Dr. Doidge, "the patterns are like a musical piece, and the neurons are the orchestral musicians that play the piece." If I am correct, there is a specific mechanism in the brain that allows neurons to communicate with each other and harmonize in a way similar to Rosenfield's players in a string quartet and Doidge's orchestral musicians.

Abundant studies have found no evidence that individual thoughts are, or can be saved, in identifiable files of neuronal arrays. One can think of the brain not as a storehouse of millions of compositions, but of billions of notes, ready to be integrated into millions of new compositions, over and again.

If all this rapid, to-and-fro electromagnetic activity cannot come to a useful consensus, a "blank" is produced, lasting just long enough for the poor owner of the vacancy to understand that he could not find a suitable answer to the test question, as was the case when I was asked for the temperature at which water boils. And when a brain is knocked about in Kenya, coherent firing of axons and their associated fields can reach no consensus at all, not even of the crash itself.

Back at work, I wondered whether I had stumbled onto a possible mechanism for schizophrenia, for which no satisfactory explanation has yet been offered. Might schizophrenia be an autoimmune disorder, like that of multiple sclerosis, causing intermittent attacks on a poor soul's internal broadcasting system? Does not the schizophrenic say that he suffers a broadcast problem, telling us that the television is broadcasting messages that he is Jesus or Julius Caesar, or, ominously, that he should kill himself? Does not the schizophrenic suffer one attack of psychosis after another until he is "burnt out," with no further attacks, though he is left hopelessly dependent, just as a patient with multiple sclerosis finally stops suffering attacks to settle into the burnt-out state of secondarily progressive disability? If schizophrenia proves to be a specific autoimmune disease, then it would be possible to block the pernicious antibody that disables moleculea on which meaningful broadcast depends. If I am correct, those vulnerable molecules would be like those described in my essay in the *Einstein Journal of Biology and Medicine*.

But let us put aside my hypothetical description of a material mechanism of thought so that we can consider another view of the brain's ability to compose and integrate. The preeminent neurologist Dr. Antonio Damasio argues in *Self Comes to Mind* that mindfulness and consciousness arise from the brain's spontaneous integration of its multiple "maps," those neural representations of both the internal milieu and the external world. The brain sends and receives messages to and from every organ in the body, maintaining an up-to-the-minute integration of the body's state. At the same time, the organs of sensation flood the brain with coded data from the external world's sights, sounds, odors, tastes, and tactile sensations.

All of this data from the body and the external world is mapped into the brain, and these maps are integrated, arranged into thoughts in one place and into emotions in other parts of the brain. And then all of these integrated "maps" of sensation and feeling are themselves integrated. "The living body is the central locus. Life regulation is the need and the motivation. Brain mapping is the enabler, the engine that transforms plain life regulation into minded regulation and, eventually, into consciously minded regulation."

Thus far, Damasio is probably correct. We do not see with our eyes alone, but with the occipital cortex, which makes "maps" from the data our retinas send in. We "see" the image we make in the dark cave of the brain. We do not see finished photographs delivered by the eyes. Thus, our mode of assembling images in the brain makes possible misperception, mistaken identifications, and even hallucinations. Similarly, we hear by assembling in the temporal lobes the information sent in by the inner ear. If our temporal lobes and our occipital lobes are damaged badly enough, we can hear and see nothing, even though our eyes and ears are intact.

According to Damasio, we live by the maps in our brains. But by what mechanisms are those maps artfully integrated? Damasio does not make this clear. How are those myriads maps integrated into new creations moment by moment? In a flash we make new worlds and new feelings. Strange it may be to consider the mind's rich and varied creations as products of transient, silent, self-harmonizing electromagnetic waves. But every thought and every feeling *does* momentarily shape itself and dissolve, however we imagine the mechanism.

I am suggesting that to make a thought, the brain marshals its electromagnetic waves to integrate its multiple "maps," themselves coded in neuronal circuits according to a process that probably resembles Damasio's modeling. However, the rapid integration of all of Damasio's maps requires a synthesizing physiology that works fast enough to give human beings the power to think and feel with human speed, complexity, and subtlety. I want to ask Dr. Damasio, how do billions of branching neurons in the brain's many divisions self-harmonize so rapidly? What language do these "maps" speak to one another, and how do they reach a harmonious consensus? And how does the holder of the baton manage his art?

Sir Charles Scott Sherrington tackled these same questions in 1940, without being able to answer them. Strangely, Shakespeare had a glimmer of the mental mechanism Sherrington sought. Shakespeare, of course, could not know about maps in the brain or anything about the mechanism of their artful ordering, so it follows that Prospero knows nothing about neurophysiology. But he does know his and Ariel's medium:

> These our actors,
> As I foretold you, were all spirits, and
> Are melted into air, into thin air,
> And like the baseless fabric of this vision,
> The cloud-capped towers, the gorgeous palaces,
> The solemn temples, the great globe itself,
> Yea, all which it inherit, shall dissolve.

The "baseless fabric" that melts into thin air is indeed as insubstantial as my description of electromagnetic broadcast.

Something like this seems to be on Shakespeare's mind. Referring to the "great globe itself," Shakespeare means that globe which sits upon Prospero's shoulders, the cranial home of the mind's phantasmagorias, all of which do shape themselves and then dissolve. The solemn temple of the "globe" also refers to the name of the theater in which Shakespeare's company acted, as well as another word for the world itself. The capacity to create the commodious idea of the entire world resides in only one fleshly place, in the theater of the human mind, which death eventually closes. Thoughts in the human globe *are* made of stuff like air, and they do dissolve by the moment, and then forever.

"We are such stuff as dreams are made on," says Prospero of the mind's made-to-be-melted phantoms. The mind's ever-changing theater recreates itself in wakeful states and in sleep, until death, the last sleep, dissolves all. Our waking life of thought and our sleeping life of dreams alike are well-crafted artifacts made from fragments mapped into the mind. Regardless of what physical mechanism integrates all the parts from which thought and dreams are made, that integration *does* occur, whether it be via the brain's own self-harmonizing electromagnetic fields or via some other material mechanism. It is precisely this kind of self-harmonizing capacity that brain injury knocks ajar, and it is this kind of capacity that can be put right by the brain's artful plasticity.

Before I conclude, let me call on Charles Darwin, who came close to offering an algorithm by which nature achieves harmony—be it in the Galápagos Islands or in the human globe. My proposal of a hypothetical mechanism by which the brain uses the broadcast and return-broadcast of its electromagnetic fields to compose a thought just happens to be a faster version of the Darwinian mechanism of natural selection, which works not in seconds, but over millennia.

The giraffe's lengthened neck is selected because it provides superior access to higher foliage, but with its head held high, the creature is at risk for overstraining its heart, which must pump blood ten feet uphill against gravity. Further, the long-necked beast that feeds on high tree branches must evolve a tough tongue that can handle thorny twigs, and, indeed, the jolly-appearing giraffe has accommodated his tongue to the demands, dishing out a tongue-lashing beyond compare. But the giant, with its head in the foliage, is an easy target for the leopard below, and the big cat, as highly evolved as the giraffe, will not be misled by the giraffe's camouflaged coat. Further, the tree cannot be denuded forever. All these factors interact until an integration is achieved, with surviving trees, sturdy giraffes, and the cagy leopards attracted to food elsewhere. Contrary to popular belief, evolution is not simply the result of the survival of the fittest, but the survival of all that fits in. The giraffe with its long neck has to evolve along with its heart and tongue, in the same setting in which the leopard evolves with its hunger and its teeth, and the tree, with its high leaves, evolves so that it can hold onto enough of them to continue with its life-giving photosynthesis. What doesn't fit in dies out.

Evolution thus executes a natural algorithm: living beings interact until a harmonized state is achieved, stable just for a time, until a new harmonized state takes over. The failure of Darwin to emphasize this natural algorithm kept most of his contemporaries from believing him. How could survival of the fittest produce the beautiful ecosystems that were everywhere apparent? Surviving species were indeed fit, but why did they fit together so harmoniously?

We can see the natural algorithm at work more clearly if we consider an example acted out on a timescale slower than the celerity of mind but faster than evolution on the African savanna. Picture a town with a thousand young bachelors and a thousand maidens living in a community that enshrines marriage. Normal human needs propel most of these blooming youths to intermingle, each man or maid signaling his or her personality and desire and receiving in return suggestive cues. Within a year or so, the church celebrates a hundred weddings, five hundred within five years, as hints about availability and reciprocation inevitably strengthen bonds. Some candidates lose interest because they are discouraged by the lack of positive feedback or because they signaled a disinterest in connubial bliss. A social buzz self-organizes into a set of stable homes, without a matchmaker, even without a God, allowing the social fabric of the town to thrive in a fecund state until the next generation replaces the now-decaying harmony.

This example of the natural algorithm creating a town of stable homes is not hard to imagine because we know what drives human beings. But it is hard to picture the mechanics of the faceless but artful brain working with an ethereal, self-programming loom. Nevertheless, a mindful loom built on the electro-mechanical principles inherent in the brain's neurons both weaves our thoughts and feelings in health, and, when accidents occur, this physiologic loom reweaves our damaged wiring with creativity, if time and chance allow.

www.ingramcontent.com/pod-product-compliance
Lightning Source LLC
LaVergne TN
LVHW012023200325
806414LV00008B/55
9781952106958